ECONOMIC ISSUES, PROBLEMS AND PERSPECTIVES

FEDERAL TAX BENEFITS FOR BUSINESS AND THE RESEARCH TAX CREDIT

ECONOMIC ISSUES, PROBLEMS AND PERSPECTIVES

Additional books in this series can be found on Nova's website under the Series tab.

Additional E-books in this series can be found on Nova's website under the E-book tab.

BUSINESS ISSUES, COMPETITION AND ENTREPRENEURSHIP

Additional books in this series can be found on Nova's website under the Series tab.

Additional E-books in this series can be found on Nova's website under the E-book tab.

ECONOMIC ISSUES, PROBLEMS AND PERSPECTIVES

FEDERAL TAX BENEFITS FOR BUSINESS AND THE RESEARCH TAX CREDIT

HARLAN VITAGLIANO
EDITOR

New York

For permission to use material from this book please contact us:
Telephone 631-231-7269; Fax 631-231-8175
Web Site: http://www.novapublishers.com

Additional color graphics may be available in the e-book version of this book.

Library of Congress Cataloging-in-Publication Data

ISBN: 978-1-62417-334-9

Published by Nova Science Publishers, Inc. † New York

CONTENTS

PREFACE

This book examines a key element of current federal support for manufacturing: tax benefits. More specifically, it identifies and describes current federal tax preferences that offer significant benefits for small and large manufacturing firms. Additionally, technological innovation is a major driving force in long-term economic growth, and research and development (R&D) serves as the lifeblood of innovation. The federal government encourages business R&D in a variety of ways, including a tax credit for a company's increases in spending on qualified research above a base amount. The current status of the tax credit is described, as is its legislative history, the policy issues it raises and legislation in the 112th Congress to modify or extend it.

Chapter 1 - Congress is considering numerous proposals to create new forms of targeted assistance for the manufacturing sector. One of the more contentious issues in the policy debate concerns the role federal policy should play in the allocation of economic resources to and within the sector. This report examines a key element of current federal support for manufacturing: tax benefits. More specifically, it identifies and describes current federal tax preferences that offer significant benefits for small and large manufacturing firms. To broaden the context for the current policy debate over federal support for manufacturing, the report also provides a brief overview of federal non-tax support for manufacturing. In addition, the report identifies bills in the 112th Congress that would enhance current tax preferences and explains how eligible manufacturers might be affected. It concludes with a discussion of the chief arguments for and against additional targeted support for manufacturing and their implications for federal policy. Current federal tax law contains nine provisions with a strong potential to provide significant tax relief to firms primarily engaged in manufacturing. A few of them are targeted at manufacturing; the others tend to benefit manufacturers more than firms in most other sectors. The provisions include the deferral of the active income of controlled foreign subsidiaries of U.S.-based corporations, the research tax credit, the expensing of outlays for research and experimentation, and accelerated depreciation for certain capital assets.

Numerous bills have been introduced in the 112th Congress that would enhance some of these tax preferences or create new ones. Among the notable proposals are H.R. 10/S. 1237, H.R. 689, H.R. 1036, H.R. 3476, H.R. 3495, H.R. 5727, S. 256, S. 825, and S. 2237. There is considerable variation among the bills in the extent to which they would benefit manufacturing firms. Several would extend and enhance the research tax credit, extend the generous depreciation allowances that were available in 2011, and allow a full exclusion for gains on small business stock.

Proponents of targeted federal assistance for manufacturing make several arguments to back their stance. First, they say the assistance is needed to help the United States become more dependent on exports and domestic production as sources of economic growth. Second, a federal manufacturing policy, in their view, would encourage the creation of more manufacturing jobs, which pay higher wages and benefits, on average, than do non-manufacturing jobs. Third, proponents point out that manufacturing industries perform the vast share of private-sector research and development, and innovation is a primary engine of economic growth. Fourth, they note that manufacturing plays a critical role in the growth of the green economy. And because many foreign governments provide assistance to their manufacturers, say proponents, the United States should do the same to avoid a loss of competitiveness. By contrast, critics of special federal assistance for manufacturing say it is not warranted on economic grounds, since there is no discernible market failure that is peculiar to goods production. They also maintain that promoting job growth in manufacturing would do little to create the millions of jobs needed to achieve full employment again. Finally, in their view, the U.S. economy would benefit more from increased efforts by the federal government to dismantle foreign barriers to expanding U.S. exports of services than from policies aimed at boosting the competitiveness of U.S. manufacturers.

Chapter 2 - Technological innovation is a major driving force in long-term economic growth, and research and development (R&D) serves as the lifeblood of innovation. The federal government encourages business R&D in a variety of ways, including a tax credit for a company's increases in spending on qualified research above a base amount. This report describes the current status of the credit, summarizes its legislative history, discusses policy issues it raises, and describes legislation in the 112th Congress to modify or extend it.

The research credit has never been a permanent provision of the federal tax code and expired at the end of 2011. Since its enactment in mid-1981, the credit has been extended 14 times and significantly modified five times. While the credit is usually assumed to be a single credit, it actually consists of four discrete credits: (1) a regular credit, (2) an alternative simplified credit (ASC), (3) a basic research credit, and (4) an energy research credit. A taxpayer may claim no more than either of the first two and each of the other two, provided it meets the requirements for each. In essence, the research credit attempts to boost business investment in basic and applied research by reducing the tax price (or after-tax cost) of that research. It is incremental in that the credit applies only to qualified research spending above a base amount. As a result, the credit's effectiveness hinges on the sensitivity of the demand for qualified research to decreases in its cost. It is unclear from available studies how sensitive that demand is. While most analysts and lawmakers endorse the use of tax incentives to generate increases in business R&D investment, some have some grave reservations about the current credit. Critics contend the credit is not as effective as it could be because of certain flaws in its design, such as a lack of permanence, uneven and inadequate incentive effects, non-refundability, and an unsettled definition of qualified research.

The 111th Congress made two changes in the credit. Under the American Recovery and Reinvestment Act of 2009 (P.L. 111-5), it extended through 2009 a provision that gave corporations the option (which first became available in 2008) of claiming a limited refundable tax credit that year for unused alternative minimum tax and research tax credits from tax years before 2006, instead of any bonus depreciation allowance they could take. And the Tax Relief, Unemployment Compensation Reauthorization, and Job Creation Act of 2010 (P.L. 111-340) extended the credit through the end of 2011.

A number of bills to extend and modify the credit have been introduced in the 112th Congress. They indicate that support for a permanent extension and enhancement of the credit remains as robust as ever. But the revenue cost of doing so and disagreements over how to pay for it are proving to be difficult obstacles for Congress to overcome. President Obama proposes in his budget request for FY2013 that Congress permanently extend the credit and increase the rate for the ASC from 14% to 17%.

In: Federal Tax Benefits for Business ... ISBN: 978-1-62417-334-9
Editor: Harlan Vitagliano

Chapter 1

FEDERAL TAX BENEFITS FOR MANUFACTURING: CURRENT LAW, LEGISLATIVE PROPOSALS, AND ISSUES FOR THE 112TH CONGRESS*

Gary Guenther

SUMMARY

Congress is considering numerous proposals to create new forms of targeted assistance for the manufacturing sector. One of the more contentious issues in the policy debate concerns the role federal policy should play in the allocation of economic resources to and within the sector.

This report examines a key element of current federal support for manufacturing: tax benefits. More specifically, it identifies and describes current federal tax preferences that offer significant benefits for small and large manufacturing firms. To broaden the context for the current policy debate over federal support for manufacturing, the report also provides a brief overview of federal non-tax support for manufacturing. In addition, the report identifies bills in the 112th Congress that would enhance current tax preferences and explains how eligible manufacturers might be affected. It concludes with a

---

* This is an edited, reformatted and augmented version of the Congressional Research Service Publication, CRS Report for Congress R42742, dated September 20, 2012.

discussion of the chief arguments for and against additional targeted support for manufacturing and their implications for federal policy.

Current federal tax law contains nine provisions with a strong potential to provide significant tax relief to firms primarily engaged in manufacturing. A few of them are targeted at manufacturing; the others tend to benefit manufacturers more than firms in most other sectors. The provisions include the deferral of the active income of controlled foreign subsidiaries of U.S.-based corporations, the research tax credit, the expensing of outlays for research and experimentation, and accelerated depreciation for certain capital assets.

Numerous bills have been introduced in the 112th Congress that would enhance some of these tax preferences or create new ones. Among the notable proposals are H.R. 10/S. 1237, H.R. 689, H.R. 1036, H.R. 3476, H.R. 3495, H.R. 5727, S. 256, S. 825, and S. 2237. There is considerable variation among the bills in the extent to which they would benefit manufacturing firms. Several would extend and enhance the research tax credit, extend the generous depreciation allowances that were available in 2011, and allow a full exclusion for gains on small business stock.

Proponents of targeted federal assistance for manufacturing make several arguments to back their stance. First, they say the assistance is needed to help the United States become more dependent on exports and domestic production as sources of economic growth. Second, a federal manufacturing policy, in their view, would encourage the creation of more manufacturing jobs, which pay higher wages and benefits, on average, than do non-manufacturing jobs. Third, proponents point out that manufacturing industries perform the vast share of private-sector research and development, and innovation is a primary engine of economic growth. Fourth, they note that manufacturing plays a critical role in the growth of the green economy. And because many foreign governments provide assistance to their manufacturers, say proponents, the United States should do the same to avoid a loss of competitiveness.

By contrast, critics of special federal assistance for manufacturing say it is not warranted on economic grounds, since there is no discernible market failure that is peculiar to goods production. They also maintain that promoting job growth in manufacturing would do little to create the millions of jobs needed to achieve full employment again.

Finally, in their view, the U.S. economy would benefit more from increased efforts by the federal government to dismantle foreign barriers to expanding U.S. exports of services than from policies aimed at boosting the competitiveness of U.S. manufacturers.

INTRODUCTION

In his State of the Union speech delivered in January 2012, President Obama stated that his strategy for economic recovery and growth "begins with manufacturing.[1]" About two months later, Gene Sperling, the Director of the President's National Economic Council, explained the rationale for this strategy in an address to the Conference on the Renaissance of American Manufacturing.[2] He argued that building a plan to revitalize the economy around manufacturing is justified by the "outsized" role played by the sector in innovation, the creation of high-wage jobs, and exports. Further enhancing the sector's economic importance, according to Sperling, were the spillover benefits of manufacturing for other firms and the communities where manufacturing facilities are located and the significant economic harm associated with a lasting loss of manufacturing production.

Statements such as these have drawn attention to a longstanding debate among lawmakers and some policy analysts over the economic role of manufacturing and whether there is a justifiable need for special federal support for companies primarily engaged in manufacturing activities. In the exchange of views on these issues in the aftermath of the President's speech, a difference of opinion has emerged that is reminiscent of the policy disputes that characterized the debate over industrial policy in the late 1970s and early 1980s. On the one hand, proponents of special government assistance to promote the growth and competitiveness of manufacturing companies argue that the sector deserves such support because it contributes more to the performance and growth of the economy than other sectors do. On the other hand, critics of such assistance maintain that what matters most for promoting increases in jobs, real wages, and output are public investments in the main forces that drive growth in the standard of living: namely, worker skills, public education, research and development (R&D), and economic infrastructure. In their view, sector-based policies are bound to fail because the federal government cannot do a better job than market forces in identifying the industries that will grow rapidly in the future and generate large numbers of well-paying jobs.

The ongoing debate over whether the manufacturing sector deserves targeted government assistance continues in the 112th Congress. Numerous bills have been introduced to provide new or enhanced federal support for manufacturing companies. Some of the proposals would do so by using tax preferences to bolster their competitiveness and encourage increased domestic production and job creation in manufacturing. These initiatives are attracting attention at a time when Congress is considering options for reforming the federal tax system as a key element of a broader plan to eliminate or substantially lower projected federal budget deficits. To critics of the current federal income tax, proposals for new or enhanced tax benefits for manufacturing underscore what they regard as a critical problem with the system: it is laden with special benefits that reduce effective tax rates and act in the same manner as federal spending, except that the spending is not subject to the scrutiny and oversight built into the appropriations and authorization processes.

To provide helpful background information for the congressional debate over whether manufacturing deserves targeted federal support, this report addresses a key component of that support: tax benefits.[3] More specifically, it summarizes the main federal tax preferences under current law from which manufacturing firms derive significant benefits, identifies the bills in the 112th Congress that would enhance those preferences benefits and how they would affect manufacturers, and discusses the arguments for and against additional targeted support for the manufacturing sector and their implications for federal policy. To broaden the context for the current policy debate over federal support for manufacturing, the report also provides a brief overview of federal non-tax support for manufacturing.

MANUFACTURING AND THE U.S. ECONOMY

According to the North American Industrial Classification System (NAICS), the manufacturing sector is composed of establishments that are primarily engaged in the transformation of materials, substances, or components into new products.[4] Establishments in this case consist of factories, plants, or mills that use power-driven machines and equipment in the transformation process. But they also include individuals who transform materials, substances, and components into products by hand in their homes and small businesses that sell directly to the public items they make on their premises.

Products made by manufacturing establishments may be finished or semi-finished. The former are ready for consumption or final use, while the latter serve as inputs for the production of finished products. For the sake of national income accounting and the collection of detailed economic data, the manufacturing sector is broken down into a variety of sub-sectors (or industries) that reflect three critical aspects of the production process: material inputs, machinery and equipment, and employee skills. The output of some industries becomes the input of others, and vice versa. For example, makers of machine tools buy many needed materials and components directly from the producers of these items, while the latter purchase machine tools directly from the former for use in the production of the materials and components.

Still, the boundaries between manufacturing and other sectors are blurred in some cases. The uncertainty largely arises from the definition of a new product, which can be subjective. For example, the bottling and processing of milk and spring-fed water are considered manufacturing activities, though they involve no transformation of materials or components into new products, whereas the erection of buildings (including the fabrication performed at construction sites) is considered a construction activity.

Manufacturing's role in the U.S. economy has changed considerably since 1960. Back then, it accounted for 27% of gross domestic product (GDP), 31% of non-agricultural employment, more than 20% of domestic non-residential fixed investment, nearly 99% of business investment in research and development (R&D), and 62% of exports. Since the 1970s, however, its contributions to GDP and employment in particular have declined.

The extent of this shift is sketched using several economic indicators in Figure 1. Basically, it traces the manufacturing sector's share of non-agricultural employment, gross domestic product (GDP), business investment in research and development (R&D), exports, and domestic investment in capital assets between 1960 and 2010. There was a decline in some measures of importance. Specifically, manufacturing's share of exports in 2010 was down 17% from its level 1960; its share of business R&D investment was 29% smaller; and its contribution to non-agricultural employment decreased by 71%. With the exception of non-agricultural employment, manufacturing's share fell because the total contributions of other sectors rose faster than those of manufacturing. In the case of employment, manufacturing's contribution declined because it lost workers while combined employment in other sectors grew, except during recessions.

Every indicator depicted in Figure 1 trended downward except one: employee wages and salaries. Labor compensation per employee in manufacturing was somewhat larger in 1960 than it was in most other sectors; the difference grew steadily until the mid-1990s; and in 2010, the gap was 7% smaller than it was in 1995 but nearly 18% larger than it was in 1960. Wages and benefits were consistently higher than manufacturing in several other sectors (e.g., construction, mining, transportation, and utilities) from 1960 to 2010.

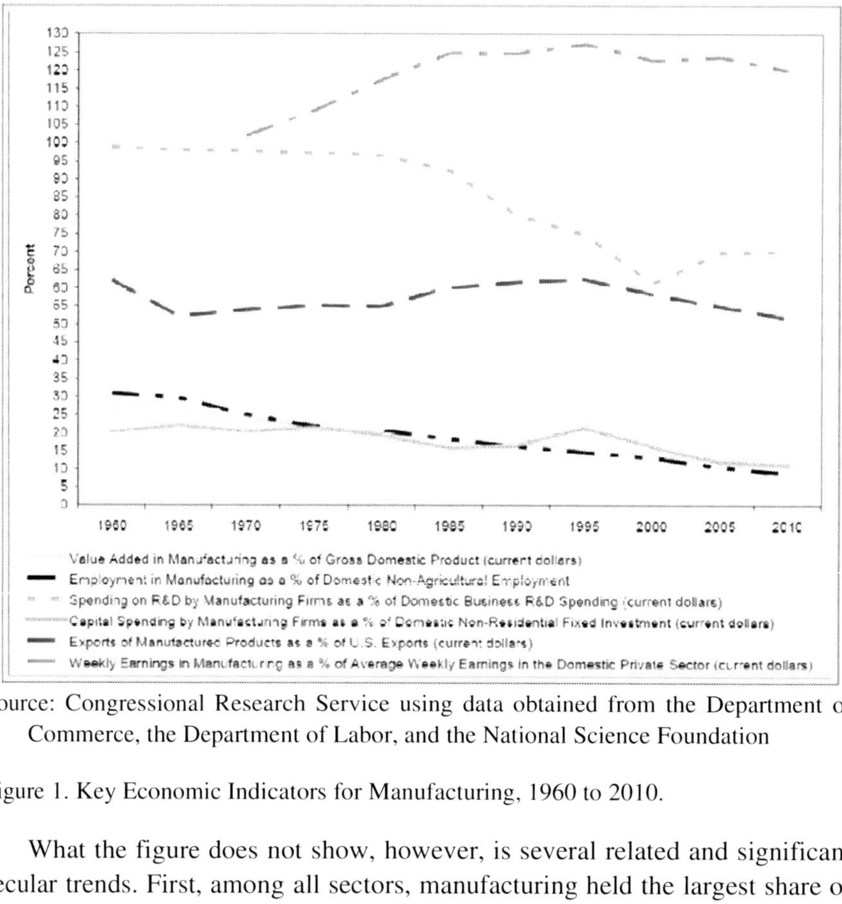

Source: Congressional Research Service using data obtained from the Department of Commerce, the Department of Labor, and the National Science Foundation

Figure 1. Key Economic Indicators for Manufacturing, 1960 to 2010.

What the figure does not show, however, is several related and significant secular trends. First, among all sectors, manufacturing held the largest share of GDP until 1986, when the government sector contributed more to overall output of goods and services (measured in current dollars).

Several other sectors have risen in importance since then, and by 2010, government; finance, insurance, real estate, rental and leasing; and professional and business services held larger shares than manufacturing. Second, manufacturing had the largest share of non-agricultural employment among all sectors until 1989, when the government sector employed more persons. Since then, retail trade, professional and business services, education and health services, and leisure and hospitality have joined government as larger employers than manufacturing.

Finally, although payroll employment in manufacturing has fallen gradually since 1979, when it reached an all-time peak of 17.985 million, the sector's value added (in current dollars), which is a measure of its contribution to GDP, grew by a factor of 11.9 from 1960 to 2010, when it reached an all-time peak of $1.702 trillion.

Table 1. Percentage Change in Full-Time-Equivalent (FTE) Employment and Real Value Added[a] for Major U.S. Manufacturing Industries, 1998 to 2010

	Change in FTE Employment	Change in Real Value Added
Manufacturing	**-35%**	**29.5%**
Durable Goods Production	**-36%**	**54%**
Wood Products	-44%	-8%
Non-Metallic Mineral Products	-33%	-31%
Primary Metals	-45%	-34%
Fabricated Metal Products	18%	-16%
Machinery	-34%	7%
Computers and Electronic Products	-40%	10,900%
Electrical Equipment, Appliances, and Components	-40%	4%
Motor Vehicles and Parts	-47%	-42%
Other Transportation Equipment	-20%	-13%
Furniture and Related Products	-46%	-20%
Miscellaneous Manufacturing	-24%	60%
Non-Durable Goods Production	**-33%**	**3%**
Food, Beverage, and Tobacco Products	-9%	10%
Textile Mills and Textile Products	64%	-47%
Apparel, Leather, and Similar Products	-75%	-46%
Paper Products	-39%	-28%
Printing and Support Activities	-38%	-15%
Petroleum and Coal Products	-10%	70%
Chemical Products	-20%	10%
Plastics and Rubber Products	-33%	-9%

Source: Compiled by the Congressional Research Service from data obtained from the Bureau of Economic Analysis, U.S. Department of Commerce, see http://www.bea.gov/iTable/iTable.cfm? ReqID=5&step=1 for more details.

[a.] Value added for an industry measures its contribution to gross domestic product. It is equal to the sum of labor compensation, taxes on production, imports less government subsidies, and gross operating surplus.

Basically, value added represents the difference between an industry's gross output (consisting of sales or receipts and other operating income, commodity taxes, and inventory change) and the cost of its intermediate inputs, including energy, raw materials, semi-finished goods, and services purchased from all sources.

These contrasting trends underscore the relatively robust growth in productivity within the manufacturing sector over that period. From 1988 to 2010, output per hour of labor rose at an average annual rate of 3.5% in manufacturing, compared to a rate of 2.2% for all non-farm businesses, including manufacturing.

Figure 1 also masks the diversity in the outcomes among manufacturing firms from 1960 to 2010. Depending on how the manufacturing sector is divided into sub-groups, many different industries could be identified and analyzed. Under the NAICS, which federal agencies use to report industry data, manufacturing consists of durable goods industries and non-durable goods industries, and they in turn are further divided into 10 major industries. The performance of these 20 industries can be evaluated using the same indicators of economic importance shown in the figure.

A comparison of the change in full-time-equivalent (FTE) employment and real value added from 1998 to 2010 suggests that some major industries grew in importance or declined more than others.[5] As the figures in Table 1 show, FTE employment fell in all the industries, but the extent of the decrease ranged from -9% for food, beverages, and tobacco products to -74.5% for apparel, leather, and similar products.

A wider and more diversified range of results comes into view when the focus shifts to industry value added. The 20 industries were evenly split between those whose real value added increased and those whose real value added decreased from 1998 to 2010. Among those whose contribution to GDP shrank, the decreases ranged from -9% for plastics and rubber products to -46% for apparel, leather, and similar products and -47% for textile mills and products. Among the industries whose contributions to GDP expanded, the increases ranged from 4% for electrical equipment, appliances, and components to a whopping 10,900% for computers and electronic products.

Federal Policy toward the Manufacturing Sector

Federal support for manufacturing encompasses a number of tax benefits, as well as a variety of spending programs largely intended to promote advanced technology development. The tax benefits are discussed in the next section, while this section provides a brief overview of the programs. As of April 2011, a total of 10 federal programs targeted assistance to manufacturing firms of all sizes.[6] The assistance involved workforce training, export assistance, business counseling, and technology development, for the most part. Foremost among current programs are the Department of Commerce's (DOC) National Institute of Standard's (NIST) Hollings Manufacturing Extension Partnership program (MEP), which provides technical assistance to small and medium-sized manufacturers to help them become more competitive and productive, and the Advanced Manufacturing Partnership program, which was launched in June 2011 and uses federal funds to leverage the creation of partnerships among businesses, universities, and federal, regional, and state government agencies for the purpose of developing advanced manufacturing technologies. A variety of smaller programs at DOC, the Department of Energy (DOE), the Department of Defense (DOD), and the National Science Foundation (NSF) also support manufacturing, mainly by fostering the development of new manufacturing technologies tailored to the missions of the funding agencies.

There appears to be no comprehensive, reliable estimate of the amount the federal government is spending on programs that support the manufacturing sector. That this is the case is not necessarily a surprise. Generating such an estimate is difficult because such support is delivered through direct and indirect channels. Direct support comes in the form of programs that either target or offer the bulk of their assistance to manufacturing firms. A case in point is MEP, which provides technical assistance to small and medium-sized manufacturing firms only. In general, it is relatively easy to determine the amounts budgeted or spent for programs like that. But such is not the case with federal programs that indirectly support manufacturing. The main difficulty lies in accounting for the value of such support, which can be defined as federal assistance that is not targeted at manufacturing but still benefits a substantial number of manufacturers.

A case in point is the research tax credit under Section 41 of the federal tax code: although it is not targeted at manufacturing firms, they are the biggest users of the credit among all sectors. But because the IRS publishes data on claims for the credit by industry and sector, determining the dollar value of the extent to which manufacturing benefits from it can be easily accomplished through the IRS website. A case in point that exemplifies the analytical challenges associated with determining the amount spent on manufacturing through federal programs not targeted at the sector is the programs administered by the Small Business Administration (SBA). While it is safe to assume that numerous small manufacturers have benefited from those programs, it is unclear how much of the agency's budget ($918.8 million in new budget authority for FY2012) has been used to assist such firms.

Nonetheless, it is possible to get a sense of the magnitude of direct federal non-tax support for manufacturing by parsing President Obama's FY2013 budget proposal for relevant programs. He is asking for $2.2 billion in federal support for research and development (R&D) targeted at advanced manufacturing technology, or 19% more than the amount enacted for FY2012.[7] The funds would go to programs administered by DOC, DOD, DOE, and NSF. Included in the request are $1 billion for a National Network for Manufacturing Innovation to be administered by NIST, $135 million for NIST-sponsored R&D on advanced manufacturing technology, $128 million for MEP, $21 million for NIST's Advanced Manufacturing Technology Consortia Program, $20 million for the NIST Centers for Excellence program, $290 million for DOE's Advanced Manufacturing Office, $149 million for NSF's programs to develop new advanced manufacturing technologies with the involvement of private companies, and $2.8 billion for DOD's Defense Advanced Research Projects Agency, which historically has played a critical role in the development of new products and processes that have had major impacts on the real economy (e.g., integrated circuits, supercomputers, the Internet).

Current Federal Tax Provisions with Significant Benefits for Manufacturing

A useful and necessary point of departure for a summary of current federal tax preferences that offer significant benefits to manufacturing is the definition of a tax preference. Such a preference (which is also known as a tax break, tax benefit, or tax expenditure) is a provision in the federal tax code that grants special tax relief to eligible individual or business taxpayers. The relief is generally intended to promote certain activities, such as the tax credit under section 41 for increasing research expenditures.

In some cases, however, it serves the purpose of assisting taxpayers facing certain difficult economic or financial circumstances. The tax relief is considered special because it represents a departure from what the Congressional Budget and Impoundment Control Act of 1974 (P.L. 93-344) refers to as "normal income tax law."

Tax preferences assume any of the following forms: (1) exclusions, exemptions, or deductions, which reduce an eligible taxpayer's taxable income; (2) preferential tax rates, which apply lower rates to part or all of an eligible taxpayer's income; (3) credits, which reduce an eligible taxpayer's tax liability;

and (4) tax deferrals, which postpone the recognition of current income for tax purposes or allow deductions in the current tax year that normally are taken in future years.

Tax preferences also produce revenue losses for the U.S. Treasury, relative to the revenue that otherwise would be raised. As a consequence, they are viewed as federal spending (for the intended purposes of the benefits) that is channeled through the tax code. This explains why some refer to tax preferences as tax expenditures. In addition, some contend that permanent tax preferences operate as entitlement programs: in both cases, their benefits are distributed or paid to qualified persons or corporations.[8]

The federal tax code contains numerous provisions granting preferential treatment to companies in an array of industries. In recent years, congressional oversight of business tax benefits generally has been limited to legislation to extend certain temporary benefits that have expired or are about to expire. Permanent business tax benefits have received even less attention. The business tax preferences from which manufacturing companies tend to derive the most benefit are listed in Table 2. Since business tax preferences are not always explicitly intended to benefit manufacturing firms in general, two methods were used to identify the relevant tax provisions. One was the share of overall use of a tax preference (as measured by the aggregate amount claimed on federal tax returns) held by manufacturing firms; the other was the nature of the preference itself, and the extent to which manufacturing firms would be likely to benefit from it, given the nature of their business.

Only one of the tax preferences arguably is designed to benefit the manufacturing sector more than others: the deduction for "domestic production activities" income under Section 199 of the federal tax code. Firms in a broad array of industries benefit in varying degrees from the other preferences, but not to the same extent, on the whole, as firms primarily engaged in manufacturing activities.

For each preference shown in the table, the following information is provided:

- a brief description of the tax provision,
- its section in the federal tax code,
- its current status: temporary or permanent,
- its estimated revenue cost in FY2012 for all firms (regardless of industry) that claim it,
- and a summary of its benefits for manufacturing firms.

Table 2. Federal Tax Provisions That Provide Significant Benefits to Manufacturing Firms

Tax Provision	Code Section(s)	Current Status	Total Estimated Revenue Cost for All Users in FY2012	Benefit to Manufacturing Firms
Deferral of active income of controlled foreign corporations	11(d)	Permanent	$14.1 billion	• U.S.-based manufacturing corporations account for a substantial share of the accumulated earnings and profits held by the foreign subsidiaries of U.S. multinational corporations. • Provision allows U.S. parent companies to defer U.S. tax on income earned and reinvested by their foreign subsidiaries until the income is repatriated as dividends. • Provides an incentive to establish subsidiaries in countries with corporate tax rates lower than U.S. rates.
Research and experimentation tax credit	41	Temporary: expired at the end of 2011	$3.1 billion	• Provision allows firms a tax credit equal to as much as 20% of qualified research spending above a base amount. • As a result, it can lower after-tax cost of qualified research, encouraging more investment for that purpose. • Manufacturing accounted for 69% of the total value of claims for the credit by corporations in the 2008 and 2009 tax years combined.
Expensing of research and experimental expenditures	174	Permanent	$4.3 billion	• Provision allows firms to deduct spending on qualified research as a current expense, rather than as a capital expense. • This treatment lowers the marginal effective tax rate on returns to investment in such research. • According to data published by the National Science Foundation, manufacturing firms performed or funded 64% of domestic basic and applied research in 2007.
Accelerated depreciation for certain capital assets, including bonus depreciation in 2012 tax year	168, 168(k) and 179	Section 168: permanent except, for bonus depreciation under	$31.2 billion	• Section 168 generally allows firms to recover the cost of qualified assets sooner than they can be recovered under the alternative depreciation system in section 167. • Section 168(k) establishes a 50% expensing allowance (also known as a bonus depreciation allowance) for qualified property bought and placed in service in 2012; the allowance was 100% in 2011.

Tax Provision	Code Section(s)	Current Status	Total Estimated Revenue Cost for All Users in FY2012	Benefit to Manufacturing Firms
		Section 168(k), which expires at the end of 2012 Section 179: permanent, though maximum allowance and phase-out		• Section 179 makes it possible for firms to expense a limited amount of the cost of qualified assets placed in service in a tax year.
		threshold can vary from year to year		• Full (or 100%) expensing imposes a 0% marginal effective tax rate on returns to investment in affected assets. • Though data on investment by industry in equipment and software are not readily available, it is likely that manufacturing firms account for a major share of total investment in those assets, especially equipment.
Option to claim a refundable accelerated AMT credit in lieu of bonus depreciation allowance	168(k)(4)	Option applies to eligible property acquired after March 31, 2008 and placed in service before January 1, 2013	Not Available	• Provision makes it possible for firms to take a refundable tax credit equal to the lesser of $30 million or 6% of unused AMT credits from tax years before 2006, reduced by (but not below $0) the sum of "bonus depreciation amounts" from all previous tax years. • It enables firms in a loss position with longstanding unused AMT credits to increase their cash flow by claiming the optional refundable credit instead of a bonus depreciation allowance that would only boost their net operating loss in the current tax year. • Historically, manufacturers have been among the industries most affected by the AMT. In 2008, mining companies accounted for 26.3% of AMT payments, followed by finance/insurance (24.2%), and manufacturing (16.8%).
Deduction for qualified domestic production activities income	199	Permanent	$11.6 billion	• Provision allows firms to deduct 9% of qualified domestic production activities income; the deduction is 6% for activities related to oil and gas production; the deduction cannot exceed a firm's taxable income or 50% of wages linked to those activities.

Table 2. (Continued)

Tax Provision	Code Section(s)	Current Status	Total Estimated Revenue Cost for All Users in FY2012	Benefit to Manufacturing Firms
				• Qualified activities encompass manufacturing, mining, film production, energy, construction, engineering, and architectural services. • Deduction lowers the top marginal tax rate on income earned from commercial use of favored property from 35% to 31.85%. • In 2008, according to IRS data, manufacturing accounted for 66% of the total value of claims for the domestic production activities deduction by corporations.
Partial exclusion on gains from the sale or exchange of	1202	Permanent	$0.3 billion	• Provision allows non-corporate taxpayers to exclude from gross income 100% of any gain from the sale or exchange of qualified small business stock acquired after September 27, 2010 and before January 1, 2013; the exclusion reverts to 50% for stock acquired on or after January 1, 2013.
qualified small business stock				• To qualify for this treatment, a taxpayer must acquire the sto-ck at original issue and hold it for a minimum of five years. • Qualified small business stock must be issued by a C corporation with no more than $50 million in gross assets when the stock is issued. • At least 80% of the assets must be used in a qualified trade or business (including manufacturing) during most of the required five-year holding period. • Provision is intended to expand access to equity capital by small start-up C corporations that may otherwise have trouble attracting such capital. Large corporations do not benefit from the exclusion.
Inventory accounting: use of the last-in, first-out (LIFO) method	491 and 492	Permanent	$4.3 billion	• Provision allows taxpayers that must maintain inventory records in order to account for the cost of goods sold to exclude any increase in the value of goods they buy or produce from taxable income. • LIFO is most beneficial to firms facing rising costs for the goods in their inventories. • Research indicates that the vast share of firms that use LIFO for tax purposes are involved in manufacturing.

Tax Provision	Code Section(s)	Current Status	Total Estimated Revenue Cost for All Users in FY2012	Benefit to Manufacturing Firms
				• Provision enables taxpayers to reduce the tax burden on the difference between the sales price and cost of inventories. • It also creates beneficial tax planning opportunities that do not exist with the first-in, first-out (or FIFO) method of inventory accounting.
Inventory property sales source rule exception	861 to 863, 865	Permanent	$6.1 billion	• Provision allows U.S. exporters an exception to the rule that income is sourced according to the residence of the seller. • Under the exception, inventory that is bought and then re-sold is governed by a rule known as the "title passage" rule. • The rule sources income from the sale in the country where the sale occurs. • Inventory that is made and sold by the company is treated as having a divided source: half of the income from a sale is sourced in the United States and half in the country where the sale occurs. • U.S. companies with excess foreign tax credits may use them to reduce U.S. taxes if they can shift income from U.S. sources to foreign subsidiaries • Companies with excess foreign tax credits can take advantage of the inventory sales source rule exception to increase the amount of their credits that can be applied against their U.S. income tax liability. This has the same effect as exempting from U.S. taxation the income that was sourced in another country as a result of the exception. • The source rule exception for inventory sales probably raises the rate of return from investing in exporting. • Manufacturers account for two-thirds of U.S. exports of goods and services.

Source: Compiled by the Congressional Research Service from figures provided by the Joint Committee on Taxation and a variety of other sources, including a compendium on tax expenditures released in December 2010 by the Senate Budget Committee. (See http://budget.senate.gov/democratic/index.cfm/files/ serve?File_id=8a03a030-3ba8-4835-a67b-9c4033c03ec4.).

Table 3. Legislation in the 112th Congress to Create or Enhance Tax Preferences that Would Benefit U.S.-Based Manufacturing Firms

Bill Number	Tax Provision(s)	Impact on Manufacturing Firms
H.R. 10 and S. 1237	• Would allow manufacturing firms to set up manufacturing reinvestment accounts (MRAs) and deduct (under a new Section 199A) up to $500,000 in cash contributions in a tax year. • Accounts would be managed by designated financial institutions with consolidated assets worth no more than $25 billion. • Would tax distributions from an MRA to pay for qualified reinvestment expenses (QREs) at an effective rate of 15%. • QREs are defined as expenses incurred by an eligible firm for investment in new capital assets or job training and workforce development. • Distributions for other purposes or involving funds deposited more than seven years ago would be subject to regular income tax and a surtax equal to 10% of the amount of the distribution included in a taxpayer's taxable income.	• Could lower the after-tax cost of investing in new plant and equipment and worker training programs for relatively small manufacturing firms. • Would add a layer of complexity to the tax code that may deter eligible firms from taking the deduction and increase the cost of tax compliance for firms that do. • Would create a form of time-limited, tax-free savings for firms that take the deduction. • Would benefit profitable eligible firms planning to expand operations more than other eligible firms.
H.R. 689	• Would permanently extend the research tax credit under Section 41. • Would raise the research credit rate from 20% to 25% for payments for contract research performed by manufacturing firms. • Would increase the deduction for qualified production activities income under Section 199 from 9% to 15% for income from the domestic production of property that was developed mostly through research conducted in the United States.	• Could lead manufacturing firms based anywhere in the world to conduct more qualified research in the United States than they otherwise would. • Could spur an increase in contract research conducted by manufacturing firms located in the United States. • Would give manufacturing companies that develop new technologies in the United States a greater incentive to produce the technologies here. • Would add a layer of complexity to documenting claims for the Section 199.
H.R. 1036[a]	• Would allow U.S.-based corporations with controlled foreign corporations (CFCs) to deduct 85% of any CFC earnings they repatriate in their last tax year before, or first tax year after, the date of enactment. • For corporations subject to the maximum corporate income tax rate of 35%, the enhanced dividends received deduction would reduce the effective rate to 5.25%: (35% x 15%).	• Would allow U.S.-based manufacturing corporations to repatriate any amount of the earnings retained by their foreign subsidiaries at a fraction of the tax rate that normally applies to such a transaction.

Bill Number	Tax Provision(s)	Impact on Manufacturing Firms
	• The deduction would rise to 100% of repatriated earnings if they are reinvested in a "qualified domestic reinvestment plan." • Such a plan must be approved by the U.S. parent corporation's president (or some comparable official) and board of directors (or comparable body). • The plan must specify that the dividend will be invested in the United States within three years of its repatriation, and that it will be used to fund research and development, "expansion of facilities, proof of concept centers, early stage venture capital investment, or manufacturing start-up costs."	• They could deduct 85% of the dividends without any requirement that the repatriated funds be used for a specific purpose. • If the results from a similar deduction that was available under the American Jobs Creation Act of 2004 are any indication, U.S.-based pharmaceutical, electronic, and computer corporations might repatriate tens of billions of dollars under this proposal.
H.R. 3476	• Would extend through 2014 the 100% bonus depreciation allowance that was available from September 9, 2010 through December 31, 2011. • Would also extend through 2014 the option for corporations to exchange any bonus depreciation allowances they could take for a limited amount of their unused AMT credits from tax years before 2006. • Would extend for three years, through 2014, the enhanced expensing allowance under Section 179 that was available in 2010 and 2011. • Would extend through 2014 the 100% exclusion for gains on the sale of qualified small business stock that was acquired in 2011. • Would extend the current research tax credit through 2012, raise the rate for the alternative simplified credit (ASC) from 14% to 20%, and permanently extend the ASC beginning in 2013. Would offer a bonus research tax credit to manufacturers whose domestic production gross receipts exceed 50% of their total production gross receipts; the bonus credit would range in size from two percentage points for shares between 51% and 60% to 10 percentage points for shares greater than 90%. (H.R. 6329 would make the same change in the credit.)	• Would temporarily reduce the cost of capital for investing in new machinery, equipment, and software through the extended generous expensing allowances. • Would temporarily encourage increased equity investment in small start-up manufacturing firms through the extended 100% gains exclusion. • Would encourage increased investment in domestic research that qualifies for the Section 41 credit through the permanent extension of the credit and the increase in the ASC rate. • And would encourage manufacturing companies performing such research to produce in the United States property developed through the research.
H.R. 3495	• Would allow individual and business taxpayers who acquire any of 10 designated manufactured products through retail purchases to claim a new non-refundable tax credit (under Section 30E) equal to the specified percentage of the total amount paid for each product in a tax year during the eligible period for that product.	• Would be likely to stimulate domestic demand for the designated products, though some of the increase may come at the expense of purchases of other products.

Table 3. (Continued)

Bill Number	Tax Provision(s)	Impact on Manufacturing Firms
	• The specified percentage for each designated product could be no less than 5% and no more than 20%. • The eligible period for a designated product could be no less than five years and no more than10 years. • A product is considered a designated product if a taxpayer acquires it as a new manufactured product for her use or lease; it was assembled in the United States; at least 60% of the value of its components and materials originated in the United States; and the Treasury Department has selected the product as one of 10 designated products, in consultation with a commission created under the bill known as the 21st Century American Manufacturing Commission • In selecting the 10 designated products, the Treasury Department should consider the number of domestic jobs that would be created directly and indirectly through such a selection, and the speed with which they would be created. • The Treasury Secretary would have the authority to specify the credit percentage and eligible period for each of the 10 designated products, in consultation with the Commission. • The credit allowed under the bill would expire 10 years after the date of enactment	• Would give U.S.-based manufacturers of designated products an incentive to acquire the capacity to assemble the products in the United States, perhaps by transferring production from offshore operations. • May to boost domestic production of affected components and materials. Would add a layer of complexity to the tax code and increase the cost of compliance for taxpayers claiming the credit and firms that manufacture designated products.
H.R. 5727	• Would extend the research tax credit through the end of 2016. • Would modify the ASC to increase the 14% rate by up to six percentage points for increases in a taxpayer's qualified full-time equivalent (FTE) "manufacturing employment." • The ASC rate would rise by one percentage point for every 2% rise in a taxpayer's FTE during the previous five tax years. • Any increase in the research credit in a tax year would be capped at amount equal to $5,000 multiplied by the number of qualified FTE employees. • A manufacturing employee is defined as an employee engaged in full-time work in qualified production activities under Section 199(c), except for the extraction of oil and minerals and agriculture.	• Would give manufacturers based anywhere in the world that conduct research that qualifies for the Section 41 credit an incentive to invest in domestic production.

Bill Number	Tax Provision(s)	Impact on Manufacturing Firms
H.R. 6240	• Would extend the research credit through 2016 and increase the rate for the ASC to 25%. • Would extend the 100% bonus depreciation allowance under Section 168(k) that was available in 2011 through 2013. • Would extend through 2012 the $500,000 expending allowance and $2 million phaseout threshold under Section 179 that were available in 2010 and 2011. • Would reduce the maximum corporate tax rate to 25% for the 2013 tax year. • Would extend by one year, through 2013, the Bushera tax cuts for individuals.	• Would reduce the after-tax cost of qualified research. • Would lower the marginal effective tax rate on the returns from investments in assets eligible for bonus depreciation made in 2012 and 2013 to zero. • Would cut by 10 percentage points the top corporate tax rate for 2013, increasing cash flow and the after-tax returns on certain previous investments. • Would prevent in 2013 an increase in the taxation of the profits earned by businesses organized as passthrough entities.
S. 256	• Would allow an accredited investor, an investor network, or an investor fund to claim a new non-refundable tax credit (under Section 30E) equal to 25% of equity investments in qualified domestic corporations or partnerships. • The total credit available to all eligible businesses would be capped at $500 million for the period from FY2011 to FY2013. • The credit would be part of the general business credit under Section 38 and thus subject to its limitations. • A qualified investor must acquire the equity or capital interest at its original issue. • To qualify for the credit, the investment must be made in a domestic corporation or partnership headquartered in the United States. In addition, it must engage in a trade or business related to advanced materials, nanotechnology, precision manufacturing, aerospace, defense, biotechnology and pharmaceuticals, electronics, computer technology (including software), semiconductors, clean energy technology, forest products, agriculture, information and communication technologies, life and medical sciences, marine technology, and transportation. Moreover, the corporation or partnership has to be less than five years old and cannot have more than 99 full-time equivalent employees (more than half of whom are performing their services in the United States) on the date of an equity investment. • The equity investments eligible for the credit would be capped at $10 million for a single qualified business in its lifetime; $2 million for a single qualified business in a tax year; and $1 million for a single qualified investor in a tax year.	• Would be likely to increase access to needed capital for some small start-up firms. • Unlike the gains exclusion under Section 1202 for qualified business stock, there would be no required holding period for the equity eligible for the credit. • Would add a layer of complexity to the tax code that would have implications for the cost of compliance and information reporting for qualified investors and the firms they invest in, as well as the cost to the Internal Revenue Service of enforcing tax law.

Bill Number	Tax Provision(s)	Impact on Manufacturing Firms
S. 825	• Would permanently extend the research credit under Section 41, retaining only the alternative simplified credit and increasing its rate from 14% to 20%. • Would allow domestic manufacturers that derive more than 50% of their total production income from domestic production to claim a bonus credit under Section 41; the increase in the bonus credit would range from two percentage points for shares between 51% and 60% to 10 percentage points for shares greater than 90%. • Would make the Section 41 credit refundable for firms with an average of 500 or fewer employees in the current tax year.	• Might allow more manufacturing firms to benefit from the Section 41 credit. • Would encourage manufacturers conducting qualified research in the United States to invest more in domestic production and hire more U.S. workers.
S. 2237	• Would allow employers that increase their total payroll subject to the Social Security tax in 2012 relative their payroll in 2011 to claim a non-refundable credit equal to 10% of the excess, which would be capped at $5 million for a single taxpayer, making the maximum credit per taxpayer $500,000. • Would extend through 2012 the 100% bonus depreciation allowance that was available for qualified assets acquired and placed in service in 2011. • Would also extend through 2012 the option for corporations to exchange any bonus depreciation allowances they could take that year for a portion of any of their unused AMT credits from tax years before 2006.	• Would encourage manufacturing firms to expand their payroll in 2012 through wage increases and new hiring by reducing the after-tax cost of doing so. • Would stimulate demand for capital equipment, boosting the output of domestic makers of the equipment. • Would reduce the cost of capital and increase cash flow for manufacturers acquiring assets eligible for full expensing in 2012.
S. 3217/ H.R. 5893	• Would permanently exempt from taxation any capital gains on the sale or exchange of small business stock under Section 1202. • Would create a limited refundable research tax credit for relatively young small businesses.	• Small startup manufacturing firms would among the main beneficiaries of the two tax benefits.

Source: Congressional Research Service.

[a] At least 10 other bills would reinstate a dividends received deduction for repatriated foreign earnings: H.R. 937, H.R. 1834, H.R. 2862, H.R. 3400, H.R. 3448, H.R. 3460, S. 727, S. 1671, S. 1837, and S. 2091. Some are more generous than the deduction proposed in H.R. 1036; others less so. Some would impose stringent requirements on the use of the repatriated funds as a condition of claiming the enhanced dividends received deduction.

Several of the provisions in the table are intended to stimulate increased investment in qualified research (Sections 174 and 41), and in equipment and software (Sections 168 and 179), by reducing the cost of capital and boosting cash flow. Tax subsidies for investment in research are considered justified on the grounds that they seek to correct a market failure that leads, in theory, to underinvestment in research by the private sector. But a similar rationale may not apply to tax subsidies for capital investment. Economists who have studied the matter have found no evidence indicating that investment in capital assets like structures and equipment is also prone to some kind of market failure, as firms are able to capture most of the economic returns. Governments typically employ investment tax subsidies as a countercyclical measure during economic downturns. The federal government did so in response to the Great Recession of 2007 to 2009 by extending and increasing the bonus depreciation allowance under Section 168(k) and enhancing the limited expensing allowance under Section 179.

With one exception, the other provisions in the table encourage the following activities: increased domestic investment and expansion by manufacturing firms (Section 199); a larger flow of equity capital to start-up manufacturing firms (Section 1202); greater cash flow among manufacturing firms of all employment sizes (Sections 491, 492, and 168(k)(4)); and increased U.S. exports of manufactured products (Section 861 to 863, 865).

The exception is the first provision shown in the table: the deferral of the active income of controlled foreign corporations (CFCs) under Section 11(b). It is the only tax provision from which U.S.-based manufacturing firms derive significant benefits that encourages them to invest in countries other than the United States. A CFC is any foreign corporation in which U.S. shareholders own 50% or more of its total voting power or the total value of its stock on any day of a tax year. Under current federal tax law, U.S.-chartered corporations are taxed on their worldwide income. U.S.-based corporations with CFCs are allowed to postpone indefinitely U.S. taxation of their subsidiaries' earnings, as long as the earnings remain in the control of the CFCs and are reinvested abroad. U.S. parent corporations pay federal tax on the earnings only when they are repatriated as intra-firm dividends or certain other income. That tax can be reduced by a credit U.S. corporations may claim for income taxes paid by their foreign subsidiaries to their home countries on the same earnings; the credit is intended to avoid double taxation under U.S. tax law of the same foreign-source income. The option for deferral and the availability of the foreign tax credit give U.S. firms an incentive to establish operations with their own profit centers in countries with relatively low tax rates.

While any U.S.-chartered corporation with CFCs can benefit from deferral, corporations engaged primarily in manufacturing seem to be major beneficiaries. The corporate response to a repatriated earnings provision in the American Jobs Creation Act of 2004 (P.L. 108-357) illustrates this point. Under the provision, U.S. corporations could take a one-time deduction equal to 85% of any increase in their repatriated foreign-source income in either their first tax year beginning on or after the date of enactment or their last tax year beginning before that date. For firms subject to a corporate tax rate of 35%, the deduction lowered the effective rate on the repatriated profits to 5.25%. Credits for foreign taxes paid on the repatriated earnings were reduced by the same amount. In order to claim the deduction, firms had to adopt a domestic investment plan for the repatriated funds. In addition, the deduction was limited to the greater of $500 million or the amount of earnings shown on a firm's books of accounts to be permanently invested outside the United States as of June 30, 2003. According to the conference report on the act, the tax reduction was intended to serve as a temporary economic stimulus measure that would not be extended or enacted again in the future.[9] In a 2008 report on the one-time dividends received deduction, the Internal Revenue Service (IRS) found that manufacturing corporations filed 55% of the returns for the 2004 to 2006 tax years claiming the deduction, and they accounted for 81% of all qualifying dividends.[10] Nearly half of all qualifying dividends were repatriated by firms in the pharmaceutical, electronic, and computer industries.

LEGISLATIVE INITIATIVES IN THE 112TH CONGRESS TO ENHANCE EXISTING OR CREATE NEW TAX PREFERENCES THAT BENEFIT MANUFACTURING FIRMS

A variety of bills to create new tax preferences that would offer significant benefits for U.S. manufacturing firms, or to extend or enhance existing ones, have been introduced in the 112th Congress. Summaries of these legislative initiatives are shown in Table 3. For each bill, the table describes the preference(s) it would establish and explains how manufacturing firms might benefit from it; provisions in the bills unrelated to tax benefits for manufacturing are not discussed.

Though the policy initiatives to strengthen manufacturing announced by President Obama early in 2012 are not cited in the table, several of the bills would each implement one or more of them. The initiatives were contained in two proposals: his FY2013 budget request and a framework for business tax reform. Several tax proposals in the budget request could have significant short-term benefits for the manufacturing sector, including a one-year extension of the 100% bonus depreciation allowance that was available for qualified assets placed in service in 2011; a 10% tax credit for limited increases from 2011 to 2012 in employer payrolls subject to the Social Security tax; and a doubling of the deduction (from 9% to 18%) for income from domestic production of certain advanced technology products under Section 199. While lacking in details, the proposed business tax reform plan would offer several benefits for manufacturers. First, it would lower of the top corporate income tax rate from 35% to 28%. Second, it would raise the Section 199 deduction for income from the domestic production of manufactured goods to 10.7%. Finally, the expensing allowance for qualified assets under Section 179 would rise to $1 million in a tax year.

NON-TAX LEGISLATION

Legislation to promote the competitiveness and growth of U.S. manufacturing firms through non-tax measures is also being considered in the current Congress. Examples include H.R. 1366, H.R. 1912, H.R. 5727, and S. 751.

H.R. 1366 and S. 751 would mandate the development of a federal strategy to strengthen the U.S. manufacturing sector, but with one notable difference: S. 751 would authorize the Commerce Department to develop the strategy, while H.R. 1366 would assign that responsibility to a commission made up of federal and state government officials and industry representatives.

H.R. 1912 would create an "American Block Grant Program" that would authorize the Commerce Secretary to make grants to governmental entities that in turn would award them to small and medium-sized manufacturers for several purposes, including investing in plant and equipment, producing clean energy products, improving their energy efficiency, and retraining employees to operate new manufacturing technologies. While many manufacturing firms would undoubtedly benefit from the support provided by bills such as these, they are not discussed here, as they lie outside the scope of the report.

H.R. 5737 would improve the competitiveness of U.S. manufacturers by requiring the President to develop and regularly revise a national manufacturing strategy that would pursue several goals, including increasing the number of manufacturing jobs so that they account for 20% of non-agricultural employment. It would also authorize the Commerce Secretary to award grants for the creation of "sectoral technology and innovation centers" to aid small and medium-sized manufacturers; authorize the SBA to offer limited loan guarantees for small manufacturers with firm orders; set funding for MEP at $130 million for each fiscal year from 2013 through 2022, with an adjustment for inflation; extend the research tax credit for three years and increase the rate for the alternative simplified credit for companies that increase their number of qualified full-time manufacturing workers; require that legislation implementing trade agreements between the U.S. government and other countries satisfy certain labor, environmental, and public safety standards; and impose countervailing duties on imports from countries with "fundamentally undervalued" currencies.

Current Policy Debate over whether to Increase Federal Support for the Manufacturing Sector

Today's policy debate over the need for more federal support for manufacturing has a precedent: the debate over industrial policy that at times dominated U.S. economic policy discussions in the first half of the 1980s. In both cases, a primary concern was (and is) the long-term economic consequences of a shrinking domestic manufacturing base in the face of growing foreign competition in global markets for advanced technology products.

In the 1970s and early 1980s, U.S.-based companies in an broad expanse of industries (e.g., steel, automobiles, textiles, footwear, consumer electronics, semiconductors, and machine tools) experienced intensifying and adaptive competition from companies based in Japan, South Korea, France, Canada, Italy, West Germany, and Great Britain.

As a result, major U.S. companies lost market share at home and abroad, leading to declines in revenue, profits, and company budgets for critical investments like R&D. Of particular concern to many lawmakers and analysts at the time was the rising competitiveness of European and Japanese companies in commercial markets for advanced technologies in aerospace, telecommunications, computer software, electronics, semiconductors, and the equipment used to produce integrated circuits. Their gains in market share worldwide gave rise to bipartisan support in Congress for several new federal initiatives to bolster the competitiveness of U.S. producers of these products, including the research tax credit that was enacted in 1981. These initiatives were predicated on the belief that some industries were more valuable or mattered more than others to sustained growth in U.S. output of goods and services and income per capita. Such a view implied that the federal government should adopt whatever policy measures are needed to uphold and strengthen the competitiveness of American-based companies in high-technology industries. The industries targeted for federal assistance in the 1980s were all part of the manufacturing sector.

Fast forward to the present. Manufacturing accounts for smaller shares of GDP and employment and was hit hard by the severe recession that began in December 2007 and ended in June 2009. The sector again is the focus of a lively policy debate. This time the main concern is not so much the potential long-term economic losses from intensified foreign competition, but the potential long-term economic gains that might arise from the federal government taking a strategic approach to fostering the growth of U.S. manufacturing companies, especially those that develop and produce domestically advanced technology products like smartphones, the latest generation of video games, and the sophisticated electronic components that enable these products to perform the way they do.

So as Congress debates the merits of proposals to boost federal support for manufacturing, it may find it useful to consider the main arguments for and against targeted federal support for the manufacturing sector and their implications for public policy.

Arguments Made for Special Assistance

Proponents of special assistance for manufacturing offer several arguments in support of their position. The arguments relate to the contribution of manufactured products to U.S. exports, the wages and benefits available in the manufacturing sector, the role of manufacturing in technological innovation, the links between manufacturing and the development and production of so-called green technologies, and policies supporting manufacturing adopted by other countries.

First, proponents point out that most economists think the United States would be better off relying less on consumption and imports financed by foreign borrowing to grow its economy and relying more on domestic production of goods and exports. Manufactured products (mainly chemicals, transportation equipment, computers and other electronic products, and machinery) account for around 65% of U.S. exports of goods and 73% of U.S imports of goods,[11] and trade in goods is responsible for about 130% of the U.S. trade deficit. As proponents like to emphasize, these shares demonstrate that manufacturing would play a leading role in any sensible policy option for reducing the U.S. trade deficit. Therefore, say proponents, the federal government should launch renewed efforts to dismantle the remaining foreign barriers to exports of U.S. manufactured products and persuade major exporting nations like China to adopt more flexible exchange rate regimes. They also call for the adoption of federal policies to bolster the competitiveness of U.S. manufacturers through coordinated investments in workforce development, equipment, software, and R&D.

Second, proponents point out that wages and benefits provided by manufacturing firms are larger, on average, than wages and benefits provided in other non-agricultural industries, as shown in Figure 1, though the gap has been shrinking over time. For instance, between 2005 and 2010, according to data reported by the Bureau of Labor Statistics, average weekly earnings in manufacturing were 21% greater than average weekly earnings in all private non-agricultural industries. And a recent study by Mark Price of the Keystone Research Center, which controlled for the key factors affecting wages such as the nature of the job and characteristics of workers, found that manufacturing workers earned 8.4% more each week than non-manufacturing workers from 2008 to 2010.[12] Not all non-manufacturing industries pay less than the average wage in manufacturing. The ones that do pay more, according to Price's research findings, such as mining, utilities, telecommunications, finance, insurance, professional and technical services, hospitals, and public administration, accounted for only 21% of total non-manufacturing workers. Price also found that low-wage workers benefitted the most from manufacturing jobs and high-wage workers benefitted the least, suggesting that manufacturing has a significant potential to lower wage gaps among workers. Proponents also note that manufacturing jobs are more likely to provide fringe benefits than non-manufacturing jobs, and that a higher share of manufacturing workers (48%) have no formal education beyond a high-school diploma than do non-manufacturing workers (37%).[13] These considerations, proponents say, demonstrate that added federal support for manufacturing could contribute to greater middle-income job opportunities and less income inequality among domestic workers.

Third, proponents cite the critical links between manufacturing and technological innovation as yet another reason why federal policy should offer special support for manufacturing firms. According to data reported by the

National Science Foundation (NSF), manufacturing firms as a whole were responsible for 70% of the business R&D conducted in the United States and paid for by companies in 2009,[14] and they employed 34% more research scientists and engineers per 1,000 employees than did non-manufacturing industries in 2007.[15] Since technological innovation is thought to be the principal engine of long-term growth in living standards and the economy, proponents maintain that the federal government should adopt policies that encourage U.S.-based multinational manufacturers to conduct more of their R&D in the United States than they already do. Commerce Department data show that U.S.-based multinational companies in all lines of business conducted an average of 84% of their R&D in U.S. facilities in 2007 and 2008.[16] But this share has been declining in recent years, as these companies have transferred some of their R&D operations to Asia in response to growing markets, ample supplies of well-educated and well-trained researchers and engineers willing to work at salaries below what is paid for similar work in the United States, and generous government subsidies.

In addition, proponents say the manufacturing sector makes a "disproportionately large" contribution to the development and production of goods and services with clear environmental benefits. A recent report by the Brookings Institution estimated that 26% of the 2.7 million jobs in the "clean economy" are in the manufacturing sector, even though those jobs represent only 9% of private-sector jobs.[17] Proponents go on to note that a number of critical green technologies and products are made by manufacturing firms, including electric vehicles, water-efficient products, energy-efficient appliances, and environmentally friendly chemical products. So in their view, a competitive, growing manufacturing sector is needed to provide the United States with the workforce skills, engineering talent, and innovative capability required to meet the twin technological challenges of producing more clean energy and reducing the consumption of energy made from fossil fuels. Proponents say that special federal assistance might make that happen.

Yet another argument made in support of federal policies to assist manufacturing is that many other countries do so, some with notable success.[18] According to proponents, the exemplar is Germany. They maintain that the federal government would do well to emulate German policy toward manufacturing, the constraints imposed by the current U.S. political climate notwithstanding. Compared to the United States, Germany has achieved better outcomes in manufacturing in recent years, as exemplified by higher wages, a slower rate of job loss, and large trade surpluses. Research indicates that these results are due in part to public policies that have fostered the emergence of dense R&D networks that cut across industry boundaries, supported a system of continuous vocational training tied to industry needs, promoted stable access to finance for small and mid-sized German companies, and encouraged the rise of a collaborative system involving unions and companies for making important decisions on issues not subject to collective bargaining. In view of proponents, the German example proves that public policy can address the basic challenges facing the manufacturing sector in ways that allow a country to achieve such critical policy objectives as relatively high wages, increased technological innovation, greater trade surpluses, improved environmental protection, and greater energy conservation.[19]

It should be pointed out that not all proponents call for special assistance to any and all firms classified as manufacturing, regardless of their size and the impact of their performance on other firms and consumers. Some argue that federal policymakers should take into account the differences in performance and external benefits among industries involved in goods production so they can devise policies that effectively encourage the migration of workers to current and future high-growth industries, remedy market failures that permit relatively inefficient firms to remain in business, and help firms with relatively low productivity to raise it.[20] To provide special assistance to manufacturing firms that are hopelessly uncompetitive, say these proponents, would end up wasting taxpayer money. Others tweak this line of reasoning by contending that the federal government and companies operating in the United States should make needed changes in their investment strategies to restore the "ability of enterprises to develop and manufacture high-technology products in America.[21]" Still others contend that government policy should provide special assistance to small and medium-sized manufacturers only since they serve as "key drivers of employment and technology growth" but lag behind large firms in adopting "new technologies that would make them more productive.[22]" Proponents of this approach also maintain that small and medium-sized manufacturers deserve targeted assistance because they face special difficulties in gaining needed public information and advisory services and play "critical roles" in supporting the competitiveness of a country's large manufacturers.

Arguments Made against Special Assistance

Not everyone agrees special government assistance for manufacturing is the key to laying a solid foundation for sustained economic growth with relatively high wages for lower- and middle-class workers. In fact, some analysts and lawmakers question the need for such support. Their doubts rest, in part, on several arguments that critics of special assistance for manufacturing have been making at least since the early 1980s. The arguments concern the lack of any market failures linked to manufacturing, the seemingly irreversible shrinkage in the contributions of the manufacturing sector to job creation and GDP over the past 50 years or so, and the untapped potential for growth in U.S. exports of services in which the United States may have a comparative advantage.

One argument rests on the absence of market failures in manufacturing. In general, a market failure is a condition that prevents or hinders the emergence of an efficient allocation of resources within a particular market, such as the market for health insurance or passenger cars. Most economists would agree that government intervention is justified when the workings of the free market do not lead to efficient or equitable outcomes in particular markets. For instance, if competition in a market is limited, antitrust laws can be used to lessen any welfare loss by curtailing the market power of the leading sellers. The main market failures involve the following conditions: public goods, externalities (positive and negative), a lack of competition, the absence of a market, incomplete and asymmetric information, and the so-called principal-agent dilemma.

In the case of manufacturing, such a view implies that federal support is warranted only if a market failure is causing inefficient resource allocations within the sector, such as sub-optimal investment in R&D or capital assets like structures and equipment. Yet some economists and other analysts would argue that there is no evidence of such a problem that is peculiar to the sector as a whole. Though they recognize there is a market failure in the form of positive externalities associated with investments in R&D that broadly affects manufacturing, they point out that these externalities have the potential to affect R&D investments across all sectors. As these critics of targeted government assistance for manufacturing note, some non-manufacturing firms, such as those involved in software development, also invest substantial amounts in R&D and thus are just as likely as manufacturing firms to underinvest in R&D relative to its overall social benefits. In their view, the preferred approach to correcting such a market failure is to do what the federal government already does: provide subsidies for R&D investment that firms in all lines of business could benefit from if they qualify.

The same point can be made about the clustering of businesses from the same industry in specific geographic areas. According to critics, there is reason to believe that clusters of manufacturing firms can be more productive than individual ones. As a result, when an investor builds a plant in an area where such clustering exists, some of the returns on investment are likely to accrue to other firms in the area. These leakages could justify government subsidies or tax benefits for the investor. But critics say that research on the economic benefits of clustering has failed to uncover such effects on a large scale.[23] They also point out that whatever external benefits arise from clustering are likely to apply in industries outside manufacturing as well, such as software development, insurance, and entertainment.

A similar objection applies to learning by doing as a source of market failure, say some critics. They note there is no evidence that the process, which encompasses the time, analysis, and adjustments required to make a new production process work efficiently, tends to prevent companies developing new production methods from reaping most of the eventual returns from those investments. If the opposite were true, then government subsidies or tax benefits might be needed to ensure that private firms continue to invest in process innovations in optimal or near-optimal amounts. But such is not the case, say critics. To prove their point, they cite a study of the U.S. semiconductor industry that found that while learning by doing was a substantial cost of investing in new production methods, most of the rewards went to the companies making the initial investments.[24]

Nor is it the case, in the view of critics, that the external benefits associated with national defense spending justify special treatment for all manufacturers. They contend that not all such firms are equally critical to a war effort. In addition, they say there is no reason why the existing U.S. production base for defense goods, supplemented by military supply arrangements with allies, would necessarily be incapable of providing adequate supplies of weapons and other needed materials during a war.[25]

Critics argue that the appropriate policy response to any underinvestment caused by positive externalities is a subsidy intended to boost investment. Federal policy does this in the case of R&D investment by funding research that most companies are loath to undertake on their own and providing tax subsidies for private-sector spending on qualified research. In the view of critics, to channel financial support to manufacturing in the absence of market failures would be to distort the allocation of economic resources among sectors, leading to lower levels of social welfare.

A second argument raised against special assistance for manufacturing concerns job creation. Some critics say it would be misguided for the federal government to direct special assistance at manufacturing in the expectation that it would trigger large employment gains over time. Domestic employment in the sector has been gradually shrinking (with a few temporary upturns) since 1979 and now accounts for 9% of total U.S. non-farm employment. In the view of critics, most of the factory jobs lost over the past three decades are gone forever. Moreover, even if all U.S. multinational companies were to stop outsourcing production and imports of manufactured products were denied entry into the United States, they maintain that growth in domestic manufacturing employment would be likely to continue to fall relative to other sectors for a simple reason: Americans are spending less of their disposable incomes on goods and more on services, a trend that has been gaining momentum since the late 1970s. Critics also note that the main cause of the sluggish U.S. job growth since the end of the Great Recession in June 2009 has been persistently weak aggregate demand. Thus, increasing assistance to manufacturing firms would do little to boost job creation in the short run, since it would have little effect on overall demand. A more cost-effective policy option for spurring faster job creation, say critics, would be to enact measures that increase total spending right away, such as tax cuts for low- and middle-income households, increased aid to state and local governments, or large public investments in infrastructure modernization and expansion.

Finally, critics say the U.S. economy would probably benefit more in the short run from government efforts to dismantle foreign barriers to U.S. exports of services than from new programs to bolster the competitiveness of U.S. manufacturers. They say the United States has a greater comparative advantage in highly skilled services such as engineering, law, finance, and architecture than in products made with the use of low-skilled workers (e.g., apparel, wood products, processed food). In addition, service industries, broadly defined, employ about 70% of American non-farm workers, and the United States is the leading exporter of services in the world. Nonetheless, according to critics, there is considerable untapped potential for expanding the U.S. share. Current service exports come from a small percentage of U.S. companies, and there is a boom in infrastructure development in faster-growing economies like China, India, and Brazil. According to an estimate by J. Bradford Jensen, an economist with the Petersen Institute for International Economics, the United States has the potential to more than double its current service exports if existing barriers overseas were removed, creating an additional $800 billion in tradable business services like law and engineering.[26] Such an increase would support or create nearly three million U.S. jobs, according to Jensen, and those jobs would be likely to pay higher wages than manufacturing jobs, on average. Given these possible gains, critics argue that the federal government should boost its efforts to press other governments to open up their service markets to U.S. companies. It should also, in their view, loosen U.S. immigration controls and work with other countries to relax theirs; such controls can restrain the growth of service exports by hindering the free movement of service workers across national borders.

Implications of the Arguments for Federal Policy

The pro and con arguments related to the federal role in the manufacturing sector have implications for how federal policy should respond to the current challenges facing the sector. The main ones are considered below.

First of all, the arguments and the evidence cited in support of them suggest there is no clear and indisputable economic rationale for providing special federal support for the manufacturing sector. Goods production as an economic activity seems generally free of market failures. Some try to make a convincing case to the contrary based on manufacturing's central role in technological innovation in the private sector, the positive external benefits associated with private-sector R&D investment, and the "direct linkages" between manufacturing and well-paying service jobs throughout the economy. But such an argument may lose some of its appeal and plausibility when one considers the steps the federal government has taken since the 1950s to lift business R&D investment to levels thought to be more in line with the economic returns to innovation. These steps include a tax credit and an expensing allowance for expenditures on qualified research. Since eligibility for these tax benefits depends critically on the nature of the research a firm conducts or finances, they have the significant advantage, relative to an R&D tax subsidy aimed at manufacturers only, of stimulating increased investment in innovative activity across all sectors, not just in manufacturing. The market failure inherent in such investment in theory affects firms in all lines of business, not just manufacturing; so policy measures to remedy the failure arguably should be targeted at all sectors.

In addition, it is unlikely that special aid for manufacturing would spark a significant rise in job creation in the current economy. The sector's contribution to overall employment has been declining for more than three decades and now stands at 9% of U.S. non-farm employment. And the U.S. Department of Labor reports that private-sector payroll employment rose by 4.267 million from its most recent low in February 2010 to May 2012;

manufacturing contributed 495,000 jobs to that gain, or 11.6%. In an economy marked by lingering high unemployment sustained by insufficient aggregate demand, increased support for manufacturing may have less bang for the buck in its impact on job creation than policy options intended to deliver a quick, sizable stimulus to aggregate demand. Examples include increases in federal spending on infrastructure, transfers of federal funds to state and local governments, or tax cuts for households. In the long run, it is economic growth that underpins and drives job creation.

The arguments also indicate that some of the proposals to harness federal policy to the goal of bolstering the competitiveness of U.S. manufacturers would have similar benefits for other sectors, augmenting the overall return on federal spending for that purpose. Some proponents of a federal manufacturing policy say it should address four major issues: increased R&D support, greater investment in worker training, improved access to investment capital, and new mechanisms for creating and sharing productivity improvements and other innovations among competing firms. There is no reason why firms in other industries could or would not benefit from similar policies. So rather than focusing on manufacturing, Congress may wish to consider cost-effective policy options for providing more R&D support, improving worker training to reduce mismatches between employer skill needs and the skill sets of workers, expanding access to credit for small- and medium-sized companies, and encouraging the growth of industry-specific networks that could offer a range of collaborative services for the mutual benefit of individual firms that would apply to all sectors.

Finally, though this issue is not explicitly addressed in any of the pro and con arguments considered earlier, Congress may want to look at the advantages and disadvantages of using tax incentives as a tool for achieving any policy objectives it may set for manufacturing industries. Tax incentives require no annual appropriations to enable them to have their intended effect. But they can operate like hidden entitlements that can impose significant compliance burdens on companies and enforcement costs on the IRS, which has been facing growing pressure from Congress in the past few years to do more with less. By contrast, spending programs tend to be more transparent and open to congressional oversight. The comparative advantages of spending programs (including credit guarantees) and tax incentives may come under greater scrutiny as Congress debates options for achieving long-term reductions in budget deficits and federal debt, including fundamental tax reform, in coming months. This issue has already surfaced in some proposals for Congress to expand federal support for manufacturing by enacting measure that involve no tax benefits. One such proposal calls for the following initiatives:

- establishing a National Laboratory for Advanced Manufacturing to undertake engineering research on early-stage applications that might be useful in a variety of manufacturing processes;
- offering competitive grants to organized groups of manufacturers and related institutions to help them to collectively solve common problems, such as worker training;
- expanding and modernizing the MEP to provide more assistance to small and medium-sized firms in designing new products, finding new markets, and distributing and marketing products; and
- providing competitive grants to companies that engage in high-wage production in the United States. [27]

End Notes

[1] See http://www.whitehouse.gov/the-press-office/2012/01/24/remarks-president-state-union-address.

[2] For a text of the speech, see http://www.whitehouse.gov/sites/default/files/administration-official/sperling_-_renaissance_of_american_manufacturing_-_03_27_12.pdf.

[3] Federal support for manufacturing is spread among several agencies and lacks centralized control and coordination. The Department of Defense funds research on new product and process technologies through its Manufacturing Technologies Program and the Defense Advanced Research Projects Agency. Under its Industrial Technologies Program, the Department of Energy enters into partnerships with industries to improve their energy efficiency through the development of new process technologies. The National Institute for Standards and Technology (NIST) devotes about half of its annual budget to promoting improved competitiveness among small and medium-sized manufacturing companies through two programs: the Manufacturing Extension Partnership and the Engineering Laboratory. NIST also supports research in advanced manufacturing technologies through the Advanced Manufacturing Technology Consortia Program and the NIST Centers of Excellence program. In addition, the Obama Administration is proposing that Congress appropriate $1 billion through the NIST budget for a competitive grant program to establish a network of regional institutes for manufacturing innovation. In addition, the National Science Foundation funds a significant share of the federally supported basic research done at American colleges and universities. Some of the research funded by NSF has applications in manufacturing; those funds are distributed largely through the Directorate for Engineering's Civil, Mechanical, and Manufacturing Innovation Organization.

[4] See http://www.census.gov/cgi-bin/sssd/naics/naicsrch?code=31&search=2012 NAICS Search.

[5] The comparison does not stretch back before 1998 because that is the first year for which the Bureau of Economic Analysis at the Commerce Department provided an estimate of FTE employment by industry.

[6] See Nisha Mistry and Joan Byron, *The Federal Role in Supporting Urban Manufacturing*, Brookings Institution, Pratt Center for Community Development, April 2011, p. 34.

[7] See http://www.whitehouse.gov/sites/default/files/microsites/ostp/fy2013omb_innovation.pdf.

[8] U.S. Congress, Senate, Committee on the Budget, *Tax Expenditures: Compendium of Background Material on Individual Provisions*, 111th Cong., 2d sess., S. Prt. 111-58 (Washington: GPO, December 2010), p. 3.

[9] U.S. Congress, Conference Committee on the American Jobs Creation Act of 2004, conference report to accompany H.R. 4520, H.Rept. 108-755, 108th Cong., 2nd sess. (Washington: GPO, 2004), p. 314.

[10] Melissa Redmiles, *The One-Time Received Dividend Deduction*, Statistics of Income Bulletin, Washington DC, Spring 2008, available at http://www.irs.gov/pub/irs-soi/08 codivdeductbul.pdf.

[11] These figures represent the average shares for the first three months of both 2011 and 2012 and are based on the latest report by the U.S. Bureau of the Census on U.S. international trade in goods and services. See http://www.census.gov/foreign-trade/Press-Release/2012pr/03/ ft900.pdf.

[12] Susan Helper, Timothy Krueger, and Howard Wial, *Why Does Manufacturing Matter? Which Manufacturing Matters?*, Metropolitan Policy Program, Brookings Institution, February 2012, p. 4.

[13] Ibid., p. 5.

[14] Raymond M. Wolfe, *Business R&D Performed in the United States Cost $291 Billion in 2008 and $282 Billion in 2009*, National Science Foundation, National Center for Science and Engineering Statistics, InfoBrief, NSF-12-309 (Arlington, VA: March 2012), p. 2.

[15] National Science Foundation, National Center for Science and Engineering Statistics, *Research and Development in Industry: 2006-07*, detailed statistical tables, NSF 11-301 (Arlington, VA: June 2011), Table 68.

[16] Kevin B. Barefoot and Raymond J. Mataloni, Jr., "U.S. Multinational Companies: Operations in the United States and Abroad in 2008," in *Survey of Current Business*, Department of Commerce, Bureau of Economic Analysis, vol. 90, no. 8, August 2010, Tables 15, 16.1, and 16.2 (pp. 221-223).

[17] Helper, Krueger, and Wial, *Why Does Manufacturing Matter?* p. 14.

[18] For an assessment of the support for manufacturing offered by Australia, Canada, Germany, Japan, Spain, and the United Kingdom, see Information Technology & Innovation Foundation, *International Benchmarking of Countries' Policies and Programs Supporting SME Manufacturers* (Washington: September 2011). Available at http://www.itif.org/ publications/international-benchmarking-countries%E2%80%99-policies-and-programs-supporting-sme-manufacturer.

[19] Helper, Krueger, and Wial, *Why Manufacturing Matters*, p.28.

[20] Ibid., p. 15.

[21] Gary P. Pisano and Willy C. Shih, " Restoring American Competitiveness," *Harvard Business Review*, July-August 2009, p. 114.

[22] Stephen Ezell, "Revitalizing U.S. Manufacturing," *Issues in Science and Technology*, Winter 2012, available at http://www.issues.org/28.2/ezell.html.

[23] Christina D. Romer, "Do Manufacturers Need Special Treatment," *New York Times*, February 4, 2012.

[24] Ibid.

[25] Ibid.

[26] Catherine Rampell, "Some Urge U.S. to Focus on Selling Its skills Overseas," *New York Times*, April 10, 2012.

[27] Susan Helper and Howard Wial, *Strengthening American Manufacturing: A New Federal Approach*, Brookings Institution, Metropolitan Policy Program (Washington: September 27, 2010). Available at http://www. brookings.edu/~/media/research/files/papers/2010/9/27% 20 great%20lakes/0927_great_lakes_ manufacturing. pdf.

In: Federal Tax Benefits for Business ... ISBN: 978-1-62417-334-9
Editor: Harlan Vitagliano

Chapter 2

RESEARCH TAX CREDIT: CURRENT LAW, LEGISLATION IN THE 112TH CONGRESS, AND POLICY ISSUES*

Gary Guenther

SUMMARY

Technological innovation is a major driving force in long-term economic growth, and research and development (R&D) serves as the lifeblood of innovation. The federal government encourages business R&D in a variety of ways, including a tax credit for a company's increases in spending on qualified research above a base amount.

This report describes the current status of the credit, summarizes its legislative history, discusses policy issues it raises, and describes legislation in the 112th Congress to modify or extend it.

The research credit has never been a permanent provision of the federal tax code and expired at the end of 2011. Since its enactment in mid-1981, the credit has been extended 14 times and significantly modified five times. While the credit is usually assumed to be a single credit, it actually consists of four

* This is an edited, reformatted and augmented version of the Congressional Research Service Publication, CRS Report for Congress RL31181, dated March 7, 2012.

discrete credits: (1) a regular credit, (2) an alternative simplified credit (ASC), (3) a basic research credit, and (4) an energy research credit. A taxpayer may claim no more than either of the first two and each of the other two, provided it meets the requirements for each.

In essence, the research credit attempts to boost business investment in basic and applied research by reducing the tax price (or after-tax cost) of that research. It is incremental in that the credit applies only to qualified research spending above a base amount. As a result, the credit's effectiveness hinges on the sensitivity of the demand for qualified research to decreases in its cost. It is unclear from available studies how sensitive that demand is.

While most analysts and lawmakers endorse the use of tax incentives to generate increases in business R&D investment, some have some grave reservations about the current credit. Critics contend the credit is not as effective as it could be because of certain flaws in its design, such as a lack of permanence, uneven and inadequate incentive effects, non-refundability, and an unsettled definition of qualified research.

The 111th Congress made two changes in the credit. Under the American Recovery and Reinvestment Act of 2009 (P.L. 111-5), it extended through 2009 a provision that gave corporations the option (which first became available in 2008) of claiming a limited refundable tax credit that year for unused alternative minimum tax and research tax credits from tax years before 2006, instead of any bonus depreciation allowance they could take. And the Tax Relief, Unemployment Compensation Reauthorization, and Job Creation Act of 2010 (P.L. 111-340) extended the credit through the end of 2011.

A number of bills to extend and modify the credit have been introduced in the 112th Congress. They indicate that support for a permanent extension and enhancement of the credit remains as robust as ever. But the revenue cost of doing so and disagreements over how to pay for it are proving to be difficult obstacles for Congress to overcome.

President Obama proposes in his budget request for FY2013 that Congress permanently extend the credit and increase the rate for the ASC from 14% to 17%.

INTRODUCTION

Economists have gained notoriety for their differences of opinion on a variety of policy issues. Notable examples include the long-term economic effects of large, permanent tax cuts; the impact of illegal immigration on domestic wages; and the best way to achieve price stability, full employment, and greater income equality. But on the issues of the impact of technological innovation on economic growth in the long run and the proper role of government in the development of new technologies, there is relatively little dissent among practitioners of what some have called the dismal science.

In general, economists agree that technological innovation has accounted for a major share of long-term growth in real per-capita income in the United States.[1] It is useful to clarify what economists mean by technological innovation, since such a complex concept can mean different things to different professions. Economists who study the forces driving economic growth tend to see innovation as a convoluted and uncertain process that embraces the acquisition of new scientific and technical knowledge and its application to the development of new goods and services or methods of production through research and experimentation. Learning-by-doing and learning-by-using often play crucial roles in this process.

In economies dominated by competitive markets, technological innovation is driven mainly by the efforts of competing firms to gain, sustain, or reinforce competitive advantages by being the first to introduce or use new or improved products or services; more efficient production processes; or more effective strategies for management, marketing and promotion, and customer service and support.

Most economists would also agree that private R&D investment is likely to be less than the amounts that would be warranted by its economic benefits. The reason for this is thought to lie in the nature of these benefits. Firms generally cannot capture all the returns to their R&D investments, even in the presence of patents, trademarks, and other instruments of intellectual property protection, and their strict enforcement. Numerous studies have found that the average social returns to private R&D investments greatly exceeded the average private returns.[2] This finding held true whether a firm invested in research projects narrowly focused on its existing lines of business, or in research projects aimed at extending the boundaries of knowledge in particular scientific disciplines in ways that had no obvious or immediate commercial applications.

Economists refer to an excess of social returns over private returns as the spillover effects or external benefits of R&D. There are several channels through which the returns from innovation may escape full capture by the innovating firms and spill over to society at large. The most common ones are reverse engineering by competing firms, migration of research scientists and engineers from one firm to another, and the availability of new or improved goods and services at prices below what most consumers would be willing to pay.[3]

When seen through the lens of standard economic theory, the external benefits of technological innovation take on the appearance of a market failure. They signal that too few resources are being allocated to the activities leading to the discovery and commercial development of new technical knowledge and know-how. To remedy this failure, most economists recommend the adoption of public policies aimed at boosting or supplementing private investment in R&D.

The federal government supports R&D in a variety of ways. Direct support comes mainly in the form of research performed by federal agencies and federal grants for basic and applied research and development intended to support concrete policy goals, such as protecting the natural environment, exploring outer space, advancing the treatment of deadly diseases, and strengthening the national defense. Indirect support is more diffuse. The chief sources are federal funding of higher education in engineering and the natural sciences, legal protection of intellectual property rights, special allowances under antitrust law for joint research ventures, and tax incentives for business R&D investment.

Federal tax law offers two such incentives: (1) an unlimited expensing allowance for qualified research spending under Section 174 of the Internal Revenue Code (IRC), and (2) a non-refundable tax credit for qualified research spending above a base amount under IRC Section 41—known as the research and experimentation (R&E) tax credit, the research tax credit, the R&D tax credit, or the credit for increasing research activities.

The deduction has been a permanent provision of the IRC since it was first enacted in 1954. Its main advantages are that the deduction simplifies tax accounting for R&D expenditures and encourages business R&D investment by taxing the returns to such investment at a marginal effective rate of zero. A similar policy objective lies behind the research tax credit, which has been a temporary provision of the IRC since it went into effect in July 1981. The credit is intended to stimulate more business R&D investment than otherwise would occur by lowering the after-tax cost of qualified research.[4] But unlike the deduction, it complicates tax compliance for firms claiming the credit. In FY2010, the combined budgetary cost of these incentives totaled an estimated $9.5 billion, or 6.5% of the estimated $147.1 billion authorized for federal defense and non-defense R&D that year.[5]

This report examines the current status of the R&E tax credit, describes its legislative history, discusses some important policy issues raised by it, and identifies legislative proposals in the 112th Congress to extend or enhance the credit.

Design of the R&E Tax Credit

Although many think of the research tax credit as a single unified credit, it has four discrete components: a regular research credit, an alternative simplified credit (or ASC), a basic research credit, and a credit for energy research. Each is non-refundable.[6] In any tax year, taxpayers may claim no more than the basic and energy research credits, plus either the regular credit or the ASC. To prevent taxpayers from benefiting twice from the same expenditures, any research tax credit claimed must be subtracted from deductible research expenses. The four components of the research tax credit expired at the end of 2011.

Qualified Research Expenditures

Ultimately, claims for the regular credit and the ASC rest on the definition of qualified research expenditures (QREs). There are two aspects to this definition.

Nature of Qualified Research

One aspect deals with the nature of qualified research itself. Under Section 41(d) of the federal tax code, research must satisfy four criteria in order to qualify for the regular credit and the ASC. First, the research must involve activities that qualify for the deduction under Section 174: namely, the activities must be "experimental" in the laboratory sense and aimed at the development of a new or improved product or process. Second, the research must seek to discover information that is "technological in nature." Third, it should strive to gain new technical knowledge that is useful in the development of a new or improved "business component," which is defined as a product, process, computer software technique, formula, or invention to be sold, leased, licensed, or used by the firm performing the research. And fourth, the research must entail a process of experimentation aimed at the development of a product or process with "a new or improved function, performance or reliability or quality."

According to Section 41(d)(3), research satisfies the four criteria if it is intended to develop a new or improved function for a business component, or to improve the performance, reliability, or quality of a business component. By contrast, research fails to meet these criteria if its main purpose is to modify a business component according to "style, taste, cosmetic, or seasonal design factors."

Businesses, the courts, and the IRS have clashed repeatedly over the interpretation of the four criteria. Although the IRS issued final regulations clarifying the definition of qualified research in December 2003 (T.D. 9104), disputes between businesses and the IRS over what activities qualify for the credit have continued.[7]

Section 41(d)(4) identifies the activities for which the credit may not be claimed. Specifically, the credit does not apply to:

- research conducted after the start of commercial production of a "business component";
- research done to adapt an existing business component to a specific customer's needs or requirements;
- research related to the duplication of an existing business component;
- surveys and studies related to data collection, market research, production efficiency, quality control, and managerial techniques;
- research to develop computer software for a firm's internal use (except as allowed in any regulations issued by the IRS);
- research conducted outside the United States, Puerto Rico, or any other U.S. possession;
- research in the social sciences, arts, or humanities; and
- research funded by another entity.

Expenses Eligible for the Credit

The second aspect of the definition of QREs concerns the expenses to which the credit applies. Under Section 41(b)(1), qualified expenses relate to both in-house research and contract research. In the case of in-house research, the regular credit and ASC apply to the wages and salaries of employees and supervisors engaged in qualified research, as well as the cost of materials, supplies, and leased computer time used in this research.

In the case of contract research, the credits apply to the full amount paid for qualified research conducted by certain small firms, colleges and universities, and federal laboratories; 75% of payments for qualified research performed by certain research consortia; and 65% of payments for qualified research performed by certain other non-profit entities dedicated to scientific research.

As a result, the credits do not cover all the expenses a company incurs in conducting qualified research. Specifically, outlays for depreciable durable assets used in qualified research such as buildings and equipment, overhead expenses (e.g., heating, electricity, rents, leasing fees, insurance, and property taxes), and the fringe benefits of research personnel are excluded. The exclusion of these expenses has implications for the incentive effect of the credit (more on this later). According to some estimates, the excluded expenses account for 27% to 50% of business R&D spending.[8]

Regular Research Credit

The regular research tax credit has been extended 14 times and significantly modified five times. Under IRC Section 41(a)(1), it is equal to 20% of a firm's QREs beyond a base amount. Such an incremental design is intended to encourage firms to spend more on R&D than they otherwise would by lowering the after-tax cost to business taxpayers of investing in qualified research above some normal amount by as much as 20%.[9] Given that business R&D investment appears sensitive to its cost, a decline in the after-tax cost of R&D can be expected to spur a rise in business R&D investment, all other things being equal.[10] The base amount for the regular credit is designed to approximate the amount a firm would spend on qualified research in the absence of the credit. As such, the base amount can be viewed as a firm's normal or preferred level of R&D investment. Two rules govern the calculation of the base amount under IRC Section 41(c). First, it must be equal to 50% or more of a firm's QREs in the current tax year—a rule that some refer to as the 50-percent rule.[11] Second, the base amount depends on whether the business taxpayer is considered an established firm or a start-up firm. Established firms are defined as firms with gross receipts and QREs in at least three of the tax years from 1984 through 1988. Start-up firms, by contrast, are defined as firms whose first tax year with both gross receipts and QREs occurred after 1983, or firms that had fewer than three tax years from 1984 to 1988 with both gross receipts and QREs.[12] The base amount for all firms, established or start-up, is the product of a fixed-base percentage and average annual gross receipts in the previous four tax years. An established firm's fixed-base percentage is the ratio of its total QREs to total gross receipts in 1984 to 1988, capped at 16%. By contrast, a start-up firm's fixed-base percentage is set at 3% during the firm's first five tax years with spending on qualified research and gross receipts. Thereafter, the percentage gradually adjusts to reflect a firm's actual experience, so that by its 11th tax year, the percentage equals the firm's total QREs relative to its total receipts in the 5th through 10th tax years. In general, the lower a firm's fixed-base percentage, the better its chances of claiming the regular credit. Furthermore, a firm can expect to benefit from the regular credit if its ratio of QREs in the current tax year to average annual gross receipts in the previous four tax years is greater than its fixed-base percentage. (See Table 1 for a calculation of the regular credit for a hypothetical established firm and Table 2 for a calculation of the regular credit for a hypothetical start-up firm.)

Table 1. Sample Calculations of the Regular, Alternative Incremental, and Alternative Simplified Research Tax Credits in 2011 for an Established Firm ($ millions)

Year	Gross Receipts	Qualified Research Expenses
1984	100	5
1985	150	8
1986	250	12
1987	400	15
1988	450	16
1989	400	18
1990	450	18
2004	835	45
2005	915	50
2006	1,005	53
2007	1,215	60
2008	1,465	70
2009	1,650	85
2010	1,825	95
2011	1,900	100

Source: Congressional Research Service.

Calculation: Regular Research Tax Credit

Compute the fixed-base percentage:

1. Sum the qualified research expenses for 1984 to 1988: $56 million.
2. Sum the gross receipts for 1984 to 1988: $1,350 million.

3. Divide the total qualified research expenses by the total gross receipts to determine the fixed-base percentage: 4.0%.

Compute the base amount for 2011:

1. Calculate the average annual gross receipts for the four previous years (2007-2010): $1,539 million.
2. Multiply this average by the fixed-base percentage to determine the base amount: $62 million.

Table 2. Sample Calculations of the Regular, Alternative Incremental, and Alternative Simplified Research Tax Credits in 2011 for a Start-up Firm ($ millions)

Year	Gross Receipts	Qualified Research Expenses
2003	30	35
2004	42	40
2005	55	45
2006	60	55
2007	210	65
2008	305	73
2009	400	82
2010	475	90
2011	600	105

Source: Congressional Research Service.

Compute the regular tax credit for 2011:

1. Begin with the qualified research expenses for 2011 of $100 million and subtract the base amount ($62 million) or 50% of the qualified research expenses for 2011 ($50 million), whichever is greater: $62 million.
2. Multiply this amount ($38 million) by 20% to determine the regular R&E tax credit for 2011: **$7.60 million**.

Calculation: Alternative Incremental Research Tax Credit

1. Calculate the average annual gross receipts for the four previous years (2007-2010): $1,539 million.

2. Multiply this amount by 1% and 1.5% and 2%: \$15 million, \$23 million, and \$31 million.
3. Begin with the qualified research expenses for 2011 (\$100 million) and subtract 1%, 1.5%, and 2% of the average annual gross receipts for 2007 to 2010: \$85 million, \$77 million, and \$69 million.
4. Multiply the difference between \$85 million and \$77 million by 0.03: \$0.24 million.
5. Multiply the difference between \$77 million and \$69 million by 0.04: \$0.32 million.
6. Multiply \$69 million by 0.05: \$3.45 million.
7. Sum the totals from steps 4, 5, and 6 to determine the alternative incremental R&E tax credit for 2008: **\$4.01 million**.

Calculation: Alternative Simplified Research Credit

1. Calculate the average qualified research expenditures in the three previous years (2008-2010): \$83 million.
2. Divide this amount by 2: \$41.5 million.
3. Subtract this amount from qualified research expenditures in 2011: \$58.5 million.
4. Multiply this amount by 0.12 to determine the alternative simplified research credit for 2011: **\$7.0 million**.

Calculation: Regular Research Tax Credit

Compute the fixed-base percentage:

1. According to current law, a start-up firm's fixed-base percentage is fixed at 3% for each of the five years after 1993 when it has both gross receipts and qualified research expenses, and then it adjusts according to a formula over the next six years to reflect the firm's actual research intensity. Thus, the fixed-base percentages are 3% for 2003 through 2008, 7.4% in 2009, 8.9% in 2010, and 12.0% in 2011.

Compute the base amount for 2011:

1. Calculate the average annual receipts for the four previous years (2007-2010): \$347.5 million.

2. Multiply this amount by the fixed-base percentage to determine the base amount: $42 million.

Compute the regular tax credit:

1. Begin with the qualified research expenses for 2011 ($105 million) and subtract the base amount ($42 million) or 50% of the qualified research expenses for 2011 ($52.5 million), whichever is greater: $52.5 million.
2. Multiply $52.5 million by 20% to determine the regular R&E tax credit for 2011: **$10.5 million**.

Calculation: Alternative Incremental Research Tax Credit

1. Calculate the average annual gross receipts for the four previous years (2007-2011): $347.5 million.
2. Multiply this amount by 1%, 1.5%, and 2%: $3.5 million, $5.2 million, and $6.9 million.
3. Begin with the qualified research expenses for 2011 ($105 million) and subtract 1.0%, 1.5%, and 2.0% of the average annual gross receipts for 2007 to 2010: $101.5 million, $99.8 million, and $98.0 million.
4. Multiply the difference between $101.5 million and $99.8 million by 0.03: $0.05 million.
5. Multiply the difference between $99.8 million and $98.0 million by 0.04: $0.07 million.
6. Multiply $98.1 million by 0.0375: $4.9 million.
7. Sum the totals from steps 4, 5, and 6 to determine the alternative incremental R&E tax credit for 2011: **$5.0 million**.

Calculation: Alternative Simplified Research Credit

1. Calculate the average qualified research expenditures for the three previous years (2008-2010): $82 million.
2. Divide that amount by 2: $41 million.
3. Subtract that amount from qualified research expenditures in 2011: $64 million.
4. Multiply this amount by 0.14 to determine the alternative simplified research credit for 2011: **$9.0 million**.

Alternative Simplified Credit

The most recent addition to the array of research tax credits available under Section 41 is the alternative simplified credit (ASC). It was added by the Health Care and Tax Relief Act of 2006 (P.L. 109-432). Under Section 41(c)(5), a business taxpayer may claim the ASC in lieu of the regular credit (or AIRC when it was available). The ASC is equal to 14% of a taxpayer's QREs in the current tax year above 50% of its average QREs in the three previous tax years. If a taxpayer has no QREs in any of those years, then the credit is equal to 6% of its QREs in the current tax year. A decision to elect the ASC remains in effect for succeeding tax years, unless a taxpayer gains the consent of the IRS to claim the regular research credit. (See Table 1 for a hypothetical calculation of the ASC for an established firm, and Table 2 for a similar calculation of the ASC for a startup firm.)

Taxpayers with one or more of the following conditions may benefit more from the ASC than the regular credit:

- a relatively large base amount under the regular credit;
- incomplete records for determining the base period as a start-up firm;
- substantial growth in gross receipts in recent years; and
- a complicated history of mergers, re-organizations, acquisitions, and dispositions.

Alternative Incremental Research Credit

Firms investing in qualified research that could not claim the regular credit had the option of claiming the alternative incremental R&E tax credit (or AIRC), under IRC Section 41(c)(4), for tax years from 1996 to 2008. The Emergency Economic Stabilization Act of 2008 (P.L. 110-343) repealed the AIRC for the 2009 tax year, and Congress has not reinstated it. When a firm elected the AIRC for a particular tax year, it had to continue to do so, unless the firm received permission from the IRS to switch to the regular research credit. There was some concern that such a rule deterred firms from claiming the AIRC, even though they might have been better off doing so.

The definition of QREs for the AIRC was the same as the definition of QREs for the regular credit. But that was where the similarity between the two credits ended. While the regular credit is equal to 20% of QREs in excess of a base amount, the AIRC, in the final year it could be taken, was equal to 3% of a firm's QREs above 1% but less than 1.5% of its average annual gross receipts in the previous four tax years, plus 4% of its QREs above 1.5% but less than 2.0% of its average annual gross receipts in the previous four tax years, plus 5% of its QREs greater than 2.0% of its average annual gross receipts in the previous four tax years.

In general, firms benefited from the AIRC if their QREs in the current tax year exceeded 1% of their average annual gross receipts during the past four tax years. Moreover, the AIRC was probably of greater benefit than the regular credit was to business taxpayers with relatively high fixed-base percentages, or whose research spending was declining, or whose sales were growing much faster than their research spending. (See Table 1 for a calculation of the AIRC for a hypothetical established firm, and Table 2 for a calculation of the AIRC for a hypothetical start-up firm.)

University Basic Research Credit

Firms that enter into contracts with certain non-profit organizations to perform basic research may be able to claim a separate research credit for some of their expenditures for this purpose under IRC Section 41(e). A primary aim of the credit is to foster collaborative research involving U.S. firms and colleges and universities. The credit is equal to 20% of total payments for qualified basic research above a base amount, which is known as the "qualified organization base period amount." This amount has little in common with the base amount for the regular R&E tax credit, except that both amounts seem intended to approximate what firms would spend on qualified research in the absence of the credits.[13]

For the purpose of the credit, basic research is defined as "any original investigation for the advancement of scientific knowledge not having a specific commercial objective."

The credit does not apply to qualified basic research done outside the United States, or to basic research in the social sciences, arts, or the humanities. In addition, the basic research credit applies only to payments for qualified basic research performed under a written contract by the following organizations: educational institutions, nonprofit scientific research organizations (excluding private foundations), and certain grant-giving organizations. Firms conducting their own basic research may not claim the credit for their expenditures for this purpose, but the spending may be included in their QREs for the regular credit or ASC. In addition, basic research payments eligible for the credit that fall below the base amount are treated as contract research expenses and may be included in the QREs for those credits as well.

Energy Research Credit

Under IRC Section 41(a)(3), taxpayers may claim a tax credit equal to 20% of payments to certain entities for energy research. To qualify for the credit, the payments must be made to a non-profit organization exempt from taxation under IRC Section 501(a) and "organized and operated primarily to conduct energy research in the public interest." In addition, at least five different entities must contribute funds to the organization for energy research in a calendar year; none of these entities may account for more than half of total payments to the organization for qualified research.

The credit also applies to the full amount (i.e., 100%) of payments to colleges and universities, federal laboratories, and certain small firms for energy research performed under contract. In the case of small firms performing this research, a business taxpayer may claim a credit for the full amount of payments with two limitations. First, the taxpayer cannot own 50% or more of the stock of the small firm performing the research (if the firm is a corporation), or hold 50% or more of the small firm's capital and profits (if the firm is a non-corporate entity such as a partnership). Second, the firm performing the research must have an average of 500 or fewer employees in one of the two previous calendar years.

Because the credit is flat rather than incremental, it is more generous than the other four components of the research tax credit.

Option to Claim a Refundable Research Tax Credit in Lieu of Bonus Depreciation in 2008 and 2009

As a result of the Economic Stimulus Act of 2008 (P.L. 110-185), corporate and non-corporate firms could claim an additional first-year depreciation deduction equal to 50% of the cost of qualified property placed in service between March 31, 2008, and December 31, 2008. The deduction was known as the 50% bonus depreciation allowance. A provision of the Housing and Economic Recovery Act of 2008 (P.L. 110-289) gave corporations only the option of claiming a limited refundable tax credit for unused research and alternative minimum tax (AMT) credits stemming from tax years before 2006, in lieu of any bonus depreciation allowance they could claim for qualified property acquired after March 31, 2008. The credit was capped at $30 million for a single corporation and was set to expire at the end of 2008. The American Recovery and Reinvestment Act of 2009 (ARRA, P.L. 111-5) extended both the first-year 50-percent bonus depreciation allowance and the option to claim a refundable research and AMT credit through 2009.

Under the Tax Relief, Unemployment Compensation Reauthorization, and Job Creation Act of 2010 (P.L. 111-312), the option to monetize unused AMT credits from tax years before 2006 in lieu of claiming a bonus depreciation allowance was extended so that it applied to qualified property acquired after March 31, 2008, and before January 1, 2013. The extension did not apply to unused research credits from the same tax years.

LEGISLATIVE HISTORY OF THE RESEARCH TAX CREDIT

The research tax credit entered the tax code as a temporary provision through the Economic Recovery Tax Act of 1981 (P.L. 97-34). In adopting the credit, the 97th Congress was hoping to stem a decline in spending on R&D by the private sector as a share of U.S. gross domestic product that commenced in the late 1960s. Around the time the credit was enacted, more than a few analysts thought the decline was a primary cause of both a slowdown in U.S. productivity growth and an unexpected loss of competitiveness by a variety of U.S. industries in the 1970s. A majority in Congress concluded that a "substantial tax credit for incremental research and experimental expenditures was needed to overcome the reluctance of many ongoing companies to bear the significant costs of staffing and supplies, and certain equipment expenses such as computer charges, which must be incurred to initiate or expand research programs in a trade or business."[14]

The initial credit was equal to 25% of qualified research spending above a base amount, which was equal to average spending on such research in the three previous tax years, or 50% of current-year spending, whichever was greater. It is not clear from the historical record why Congress chose a statutory rate of 25%. But there is no evidence that the rate was chosen on the basis of a rigorous assessment of the gap between the private and social returns to R&D investment, or the sensitivity of R&D expenditures to declines in their after-tax cost. Any taxpayer that claimed the credit and could not apply the entire amount against its current-year federal income tax liability was allowed to carry the unused portion back as many as three tax years, or forward as many as 15 tax years. The credit was to remain in effect from July 1, 1981, to December 31, 1985.

Congress made the first significant changes in the original research tax credit with the passage of the Tax Reform Act of 1986 (TRA86, P.L. 99-514). Among the many significant changes it made in the federal tax code, the act extended the credit through December 31, 1988, and folded it into the general business credit under IRC Section 38, thereby subjecting it to a yearly cap. In addition, the act lowered the credit's statutory rate to 20%, modified the definition of QREs so that the credit applied to research intended to produce new technical knowledge deemed useful in the commercial development of new products and processes, and created a separate 20% incremental tax credit for payments to universities and certain other nonprofit organizations for the conduct of basic research according to a written contract. The reduction in the credit's rate seemingly was not based on an analysis of the credit's effectiveness in the first five years. Rather, it seemed to stem from the overriding goals of TRA86, which were to lower income tax rates across the board, broaden the income tax base, and shrink the differences in tax burdens among major categories of business investments. Since 1954, firms investing in R&D had already been benefiting from the option to expense qualified R&D spending under the IRC Section 174 expensing allowance.[15]

The regular and basic research credits were further altered by the Technical and Miscellaneous Revenue Act of 1988 (P.L. 100-647). Specifically, the act extended the credits through December 31, 1989. It also curtailed the overall tax preference for private-sector R&D investment by requiring business taxpayers to reduce any deduction they claim for research spending under IRC Section 174 by half of the sum of any regular and basic research credits they claim. This new rule decreased the maximum effective rate of the regular research tax credit by a factor equal to 0.5 times a taxpayer's marginal income tax rate.[16]

Continuing disappointment with the design of the original credit among interested parties led to the enactment of several additional changes in the regular credit through the Omnibus Budget Reconciliation Act of 1989 (OBRA89, P.L. 101-239). Much of the disappointment was focused on the formula for determining the base amount of the credit. Critics rightly pointed out that under the formula, which was based on a three-year moving average of a firm's annual spending on qualified research, an increase in a firm's research spending in one year would raise its base amount in each of the following three years by an amount equal to one-third of that increase, possibly making it more difficult to claim the credit in those three years. Some argued that such a design would be less cost-effective in boosting business R&D investment than one in which a firm's base amount was completely independent of its current spending on qualified research.[17]

To address this concern, OBRA89 changed the formula for the base amount so that it was equal to the greater of 50% of a firm's current-year QREs, or the product of the firm's average annual gross receipts in the previous four tax years and a "fixed-base percentage." The act set this percentage equal to the ratio of a firm's total QREs to total gross receipts in the four tax years from 1984 to 1988, capped at 16%. OBRA89 also made the credit available on more favorable terms to start-up firms, which it defined as firms without gross receipts and QREs in three of the four years from 1984 to 1988; these firms were assigned a fixed base percentage of 3%. In addition, the act effectively extended the credits to December 31, 1990 (by requiring that QREs incurred before January 1, 1991, be prorated), made it clear that firms could apply the regular credit to QREs related to current lines of business and possible future lines of business, and required firms claiming the regular and basic research credits to reduce any deduction they claim under IRC Section 174 by the entire amount of the credits.

In 1990 and 1991, Congress passed two bills that, among other things, temporarily extended the credits. The Omnibus Budget Reconciliation Act of 1990 (P.L. 101-508) extended the credits through December 31, 1991, and repealed the requirement that QREs made before January 1, 1991, be prorated. And the Tax Extension Act of 1991 (P.L. 102-227) pushed the expiration date for the credits forward to June 30, 1992. A major obstacle to longer extensions of the credits at the time lay in congressional budget rules requiring that the revenue cost of lengthy or permanent extensions be scored over 10 fiscal years and offset with tax increases or cuts in non-defense discretionary spending.

Although Congress passed two bills in 1992 that would have extended the credits beyond June 30 of that year, President George H. W. Bush vetoed both for reasons that had nothing to do with the credit provisions. As a result, the credits expired and remained unavailable from July 1, 1992, until the enactment of the Omnibus Budget Reconciliation Act of 1993 (OBRA93, P.L. 103-66) in August 1993. That act extended the credits retroactively from July 1, 1992, through June 30, 1995. It also modified the fixed-base percentage for start-up firms. Specifically, a firm lacking gross receipts in three of the years from 1984 to 1988 was assigned a percentage of 3% for the first five tax years after 1993 in which it reported QREs. Starting in the sixth year, the percentage was to adjust gradually so that by the 11th year the percentage would reflect its actual ratio of total QREs to total gross receipts in five of the previous six tax years.

Congressional inaction allowed the credits to expire again on June 30, 1995. They remained in abeyance until the enactment of the Small Business Job Protection Act of 1996 (P.L. 104-188) in August 1996. That act retroactively reinstated the credits from July 1, 1996, to May 31, 1997, leaving a one-year gap in the credit's coverage since its inception in mid-1981. The act also expanded the definition of a start-up firm to include any firm whose first tax year with both gross receipts and QREs was 1984 or later, added a three-tiered alternative incremental research credit (AIRC) with initial rates of 1.65%, 2.2%, and 2.75%, and made 75% of payments for qualified research performed under contract by nonprofit organizations "operated primarily to conduct scientific research" eligible for the regular credit and the AIRC.

The credits expired again in 1997, but they were extended retroactively from June 1, 1997, to June 30, 1998, by the Taxpayer Relief Act of 1997 (P.L. 105-34). A further extension of the credits to June 30, 1999, was included in the revenue portion of the Omnibus Consolidated and Emergency Supplemental Appropriations Act, 1998 (P.L. 105-277).

Under circumstances reminiscent of 1997, the credits expired in 1999. But the revenue portion of the Ticket to Work and Work Incentives Improvement Act of 1999 (P.L. 106-170) extended them from July 1, 1999, to June 30, 2004. It also increased the three rates of the AIRC to 2.65%, 3.2%, and 3.75% and expanded the definition of qualified research to include qualified research performed in Puerto Rico and the other territorial possessions of the United States.

On October 4, 2004, President George W. Bush signed into law the Working Families Tax Relief Act of 2004 (P.L. 108-311), which included a provision extending the research tax credit through December 31, 2005.

The Energy Policy Act of 2005 (P.L. 109-58) added a fourth component to the research tax credit by establishing a credit equal to 20% of payments for energy research performed under contract by qualified research consortia, colleges and universities, federal laboratories, and eligible small firms.

Under the Tax Relief and Health Care Act of 2006 (P.L. 109-432), the research tax credit was extended retroactively through the end of 2007. The act also raised the three rates for the AIRC to 3%, 4%, and 5%, and established yet another research tax credit, known as the alternative simplified credit (ASC). This fifth component of the credit was equal to 12% of QREs in excess of 50% of average QREs in the past three tax years; for business taxpayers with no QREs in any of the three preceding tax years, the credit was equal to 6% of QREs in the current tax year.

The Emergency Economic Stabilization Act of 2008 (P.L. 110-343) retroactively extended the research credit through 2009. It also raised the rate of the ASIC from 12% to 14% and repealed the AIRC for the 2009 tax year only. Under the Housing and Economic Recovery Act of 2008 (P.L. 110-289), corporations gained the option for the 2008 tax year only of claiming a limited refundable credit for unused research and AMT credits from tax years before 2006, in lieu of any bonus depreciation allowance they could claim for qualified assets placed in service between March 31, 2008, and December 31, 2008. The American Recovery and Reinvestment Act of 2009 (P.L. 111-5) extended that option through 2009, along with the bonus depreciation allowance that applied in 2008. As a result of the Tax Relief, Unemployment Compensation Reauthorization, and Job Creation Act of 2010, (P.L. 111-312), the research credit was extended through 2011.

Going back to the mid-1990s, a discernible cycle seems to emerge every time the credit is about to expire. The cycle commences when congressional and business supporters of the credit issue public statements calling for a permanent extension of the credit and denouncing what they see as the folly of repeated temporary extensions.[18] Then the President in office when the cycle begins expresses his support for such an extension. In the next stage of the cycle, leaders in both houses of Congress enter into negotiations on tax legislation that includes a permanent extension of the credit. But in the end, Congress and the President can agree only on a limited extension of the credit, stymied by the difficulty of reconciling the revenue cost of a permanent extension with other budget priorities. It remains to be seen if this cycle reappears in the efforts by the Congress and President Obama to reach an agreement on a plan to reduce or eliminate projected federal budget deficits over the next two decades.

EFFECTIVENESS OF THE RESEARCH TAX CREDIT

For analysts and lawmakers alike, probably the most important policy issue raised by the research tax credit is its effectiveness. Basically, there are two approaches to assessing this critical aspect of the credit.

Among economists, the preferred approach is to compare the social benefits from any added qualified research induced by the credit with the social costs of that research. Such an undertaking involves comparing the returns to society of the additional qualified research spending associated with the credit to the opportunity costs to society of those outlays. The social cost of the credit can be thought of as the net loss of tax revenue because of the credit, together with the public and private costs of administering the credit. Unfortunately, this approach has little application in policymaking, largely because it is difficult to measure accurately the social returns to R&D.[19]

As a result, economists have relied on the next best approach: estimating the additional qualified research (if any) stimulated by the regular credit, and comparing the dollar value of that gain with the tax revenue lost because of the credit. Such an approach compares the direct benefits (i.e., added research investment) with the direct costs (revenue loss) of the regular credit. It presupposes that the social returns to the research far exceed the private returns, and that the optimal size of any tax subsidy for R&D can be estimated. If the ratio of benefits to cost is greater than one, then the credit can be seen as a more cost-effective way to boost research than direct research subsidies; if it is less than one, then funding the research directly would be more cost-effective.[20]

What do available studies say about the effectiveness of the regular research credit? Going back to the early days of the credit, economists who have evaluated its impact on business investment in qualified research have used a variety of methods to estimate the amount of additional research that can be attributed to the credit. These methods were reviewed in a 1995 study by economist Bronwyn Hall.[21] She found that the studies using data on the credit from 1981 to 1983 came up with lower estimates of the added research associated with one dollar of the credit than did the studies based on data from 1984 and after. Taking into consideration the strengths and weaknesses of the studies, Hall concluded that the credit led to a "dollar-for-dollar increase in reported R&D spending on the margin."[22] In other words, over the period (mid-to-late 1980s) covered by the later studies, she found that one dollar of the credit resulted in a company spending an additional dollar on qualified research, suggesting that the credit was as cost-effective as federal research grants.

STIMULATIVE EFFECT OF THE CREDIT

What does available evidence say about the stimulative effect of the credit? This effect refers to the percentage increase in research spending over a period that can be attributed to the credit. Answering the question entails applying what is known about the responsiveness of business spending on research to declines in its tax price to the reduction in the aggregate cost of research that could be due to the credit.

In theory, the credit stimulates increased investment in qualified research by lowering the after-tax cost of undertaking another dollar of that research. In other words, the credit lowers the tax price of research, and firms respond to the lower prices by spending more on it, all other things being equal. Early studies of the responsiveness of research spending to price decreases estimated that the tax price elasticity of demand for research was less than one, perhaps somewhere between -0.2 to -0.5. This meant that a 10% reduction in the after-tax (or net) cost of research should lead to an increase in research spending of 2% to 5%. More recent studies, however, indicated that research spending probably has a stronger sensitivity to price changes. On the whole, they suggested that the tax price elasticity was closer to -1.0 in the short run, which meant that a 10% reduction in the cost of research would trigger a 10% rise in research spending. Several of the studies also concluded that research tax credits may have an even larger impact on research spending in the longer run, on the order of -2.0. Still, the question of how responsive the demand for research is to tax price decreases remains open to further debate and analysis, as available studies have data and methodological limitations that cast doubt on the validity of their estimates. In an assessment of the revenue effects of President Bush's FY2004 budget request, the Joint Committee on Taxation (JCT) noted that "the general consensus when assumptions are made with respect to research expenditures is that the price elasticity of research is less than -1.0 and may be less than -0.5."[23] Therefore, for the sake of this analysis, it seems reasonable to assume that the actual price elasticity for qualified research lies between -0.4 and -0.8.

A measure of the reduction in the cost of aggregate qualified research that may be due to the credit is its average effective rate. The rate captures the percentage reduction in that cost because of the credit. It is derived by dividing the total amount of claims for the research credit in a tax year by some measure of total business spending on qualified research in the same year. There are two such measures: QREs, as reported by the IRS, and industry spending on basic and applied research and development, as reported by the National Science Foundation (NSF). As a result, the rate can be computed for both QREs and business investment in R&D. As Table 3 shows, the average effective rate of the credit from 1998 to 2008 was 3.3% for business investment in R&D and 5.3% for QREs.

Table 3. U.S. Business Research Spending, Federal Spending on Research and Development, and Claims for the Federal Research Tax Credit, 1998 to 2008 ($ billions)

	1998	1999	2000	2001	2002	2003	2004	2005	2006	2007	2008
Business Spending on R&D (BSRD)[a]	$145.0	$161.6	$182.8	$185.1	$177.5	$182.9	$188.0	$204.2	$223.4	$242.7	$263.3
Qualified Research Spending (QRS)[b]	$95.9	$102.7	$109.9	$99.8	$116.1	$124.5	$116.1	$129.8	$144.7	$158.1	$150.8
Federal R&D Spending[c]	$73.6	$77.6	$78.7	$86.8	$97.6	$112.5	$121.9	$126.6	$131.6	$138.1	$138.0
Current-Year Research Tax Credit[d]	$5.3	$5.3	$7.2	$6.4	$5.7	$5.5	$5.6	$6.4	$7.3	$8.3	$8.3
Ratio of Credit to BSRD (%)	3.6%	3.3%	3.9%	3.5%	3.2%	3.0%	3.0%	3.1%	3.3%	3.4%	3.1%
Ratio of Credit to QRS (%)	5.5%	5.2%	6.5%	6.4%	4.9%	4.4%	4.8%	4.9%	5.0%	5.2%	5.5%

Source: National Science Foundation, Division of Science Resources Statistics, *InfoBrief: Increase in U.S. Industrial R&D Expenditures Reported for 2003 Makes Up For Earlier Decline*; National Science Foundation, Division of Science Resources Statistics, *Survey of Federal Funds for Research and Development: Fiscal Years 2000, 2001, and 2002*; Internal Revenue Service, Statistics of Income Division, e-mail data transmissions.

a. Total spending on domestic basic and applied research by companies.

b. Spending on research that qualifies for the regular, alternative incremental, and university basic research tax credits, as reported by corporations claiming the credit on their federal income tax returns.

c. Budget authority for Federal defense and non-defense R&D spending by fiscal year.

d. Total value of claims for the regular, incremental and basic research tax credits reported in federal corporate income tax returns. Because of limitations on the use of the general business credit, of which the research credit is a component, and audits of corporate claims for the credit by the Internal Revenue Service, the total amount of the research credit actually used in a particular year may differ from the total amount claimed.

This implies that the credit lowered the after-tax cost of research (which may or may not qualify for the credit) between 3.3% and 5.3%, on average, during that decade.

The gap between the rates largely reflects the difference in the scope of QREs and business R&D spending, as estimated by the NSF. Aggregate QREs amounted to 62.3% of aggregate business R&D spending from 1998 to 2008. The NSF estimate covers domestic R&D funded by firms. It is based on annual surveys of business R&D and takes into account the wages, salaries, and fringe benefits of research personnel; the cost of materials and supplies, overhead expenses; and depreciation related to research activities. Excluded from the estimate are expenditures on the buildings and equipment used in research, quality control, routine product testing, and production.[24] By contrast, QREs represent total spending on research that is eligible for the credit, as reported to the IRS on Form 6765; they cover the wages and salaries of research personnel; materials, supplies, and leased computer time used in qualified research; and 65% to 75% of contract research funded by the taxpayers claiming the credit. Since the NSF numbers cover more of the cost of business investment in R&D, they should be larger than the QREs for the same years. What is unclear is the extent to which the NSF figures exceed the QREs reported to the IRS.

The figures in Table 3 suggest that the credit delivered no more than a modest stimulus to domestic business R&D investment from 1998 to 2008. Specifically, assuming the price elasticity of demand for qualified research lies between -0.4 and -0.8, and the credit lowers the net cost of business spending on qualified research by 5.3%, one can argue the credit may have boosted that spending somewhere between 2.1% (0.4 x 5.3%) and 4.2% (0.8 x 5.3%), compared with the investment that would likely have taken place without the credit.[25]

POLICY ISSUES RAISED BY THE CURRENT RESEARCH TAX CREDIT

Many policy analysts and lawmakers endorse the use of tax incentives to spur increased business R&D investment. Yet the current research tax credit sometimes seems to attract more words of criticism than praise. The main concern of critics is that the credit has not been as effective as it should have because of what they say are certain problems with its design. In their view, the credit can yield its intended benefits only if it is altered to remedy five problems in particular: (1) the credit is not a permanent provision of the IRC; (2) it still has weak and uneven incentive effects; (3) it is not refundable; (4) the definition of qualified research remains incomplete and ambiguous, and thus a major source of disputes between the IRS and taxpayers; and (5) the credit is not targeted at investments that are likely to generate relatively large economic benefits. Each problem is discussed in some depth below.

Lack of Permanence

The research tax credit has never been a permanent provision of the IRC, despite repeated attempts in Congress to extend it permanently in the past decade.[26] In fact, the credit has now been extended 14 times, most recently by the Tax Relief, Unemployment Compensation Reauthorization, and Job Creation Act of 2010.

This lack of permanence is a cause for concern to many because it is thought to weaken the credit's incentive effect. Many R&D projects have planning horizons that extend beyond a year or two. If business managers cannot count on receiving the credit over the expected life of an R&D project, they are unlikely to take it into account when setting the size of annual R&D budgets. Under these circumstances, the credit would exert little or no influence over R&D investment decisions, defeating its purpose. Instead of boosting R&D investment, a temporary research tax credit could end up restraining it by compounding the uncertainty that typically characterizes projected after-tax returns on planned R&D investments, and by keeping the cost of capital for such investments higher than it otherwise would be. A combination of added uncertainty and larger capital costs may deter managers from pursuing some of the R&D projects they would undertake if the credit were permanent.

Still, it seems unlikely that all firms investing in R&D would be affected in the same manner by a temporary research tax credit. Firms with relatively long R&D planning horizons and relatively high fixed costs for R&D investment might show more sensitivity to uncertainty in the availability of a credit than firms with shorter horizons and relatively low fixed investment costs. For example, it is conceivable (though hard to prove) that a string of temporary credits may lead pharmaceutical firms to expand their research budgets slower than software firms, simply because pharmaceutical R&D

projects, on average, have longer planning horizons and require greater investments in plant and equipment than software R&D projects do.

Uneven and Inadequate Incentive Effects

Critics maintain that another significant problem with the research tax credit is its incentive effect. A credit's incentive effect refers to the size of the benefit it offers eligible taxpayers. In the view of critics, the research credit's incentive effect varies among firms conducting qualified research in ways that are not supported by economic theory and can even defeat the credit's purpose. In addition, they contend that this incentive effect is too meager to offset the inclination of firms to invest less in research than its potential spillover benefits warrant. To what extent can it be said that the credit's incentive effect is too uneven and small?

Uneven Incentive Effect

The regular credit's incentive effect appears to vary widely among firms investing in qualified research, including those that gradually increase their research investment over an extended period. Evidence for such variation can be found in a number of sources, including a 1996 study by economist William Cox that estimated which of a large group of domestic corporations with sizable research budgets in 1994 should have be able to claim the regular credit.

The study was based on a sample of 900 publicly traded U.S.-based firms with the largest R&D budgets, culled from a database maintained by Compustat, Inc. Under the reasonable assumption that QREs for these firms were equal to 70% of their reported R&D spending for 1994, Cox determined that 62.5% of the firms could be considered established firms for the purpose of claiming the regular credit, as they had both business revenue and QREs in three of the years from 1984 to 1988; the remainder were treated as start-up firms. Cox found that 78% of the 900 firms in the sample (44.4% of the established firms and 33.5% of the start-up firms) could have claimed the credit in 1994, while 22% could have claimed no credit (18% of established firms and 4% of start-up firms).[27] He also found that 34% of all firms (32.3% of established firms and 1.7% of start-up firms) had QREs greater than their base amounts but less than twice those amounts, allowing them to claim credits with a marginal effective rate of 13%, and that 43.8% of all firms had QREs greater than double their base amounts, allowing them to claim credits with a marginal effective rate of 6.5%.[28] These rates measure the reduction in the after-tax cost of qualified research as a result of taking the regular credit. In addition, Cox found that some of the most research-intensive firms could claim either no credit or credits with a marginal effective rate half as large as the rate for the credits that could be claimed by firms with much lower propensity to invest in research.

The results seemed to confirm that the regular credit was most beneficial to firms whose research intensities had grown since their base periods and least beneficial to firms whose research intensities had changed little or not at all or had shrunk since their base periods. Most of the firms whose research intensities had declined found themselves in that position for two reasons: (1) their R&D spending was lower in 1994 than it was in their base period, or (2) their sales revenue had grown faster than their R&D expenditures over the same period.

Critics of the design of the regular credit argue that the pattern of R&D subsidization found in the Cox study is unfair and arbitrary, has no justification in standard economic theory, and undercuts the intended purpose of the credit, which is to encourage all firms to spend more on R&D than they otherwise would. Cox said as much when he concluded that the wide variation in the marginal effective rates of the credit among the firms in his analysis suggested "that society places a higher value on adding R&D at certain firms than at others and on adding R&D of certain types than others, when little or no basis for such different valuations exists."[29]

Two rules governing the use of the regular credit are responsible for most of the variation in its incentive effect. One is the requirement that the base amount for the regular credit cannot be less than 50% of QREs. The other rule is the requirement that established firms use gross receipts and QREs from 1984 to 1988 to calculate their fixed-base percentages.

In combination, the rules can produce remarkably dissimilar outcomes in the use of the regular credit among firms that spend substantial amounts on qualified research. Of particular concern to critics are firms whose research-intensity (as measured by spending on R&D as a share of revenue) has shrunk over time. The structure of the U.S. economy can and does change markedly in a period of 20 or so years. So it is likely that economic and competitive conditions in research-intensive industries today bear little resemblance to the conditions that prevailed in the 1980s. Most of the firms that have remained in business as independent entities and invested considerable amounts in R&D relative to revenues since then face much different climates for R&D investment. In some cases, the change in circumstances has led established firms to invest less in R&D as a share of revenues. Firms in this position may not be able to claim the regular credit, even if they spend relatively large sums on R&D.[30]

Inadequate Incentive Effect

In claiming that the regular credit's incentive effect is inadequate, critics actually have in mind two different measures of the effect. One deals with the credit rate deemed essential to coaxing companies to increase their R&D investments to socially optimal levels; the other concerns differences between the regular credit's statutory rate and its average marginal effective rate. Both measures are examined here.

Research Credit Rate and Socially Optimal Levels of Investment in Research

Critics maintain that the average effective rate of the regular credit is too low to support levels of business investment in research commensurate with its economic benefits. To substantiate this contention, they point to another study by Cox, one that focused on the efficacy of the research tax credit.[31] Cox built the analysis around the premise that tax incentives can overcome the private sector's inclination to invest too little in the creation of new technical knowledge and know-how. For tax incentives to have this effect, they must be designed so they subsidize R&D spending above and beyond what firms would undertake on their own, and they must be large enough to "raise private after-tax returns on R&D investments to the levels that would result from applying the same rate of taxation to the social rate of return from R&D."[32] A variety of studies from the past 50 years or so have concluded that the median private rate of return on R&D investment is roughly 50% of the median social rate of return.[33] Thus, assuming that the average social pre-tax rate of return is two times the average private pre-tax rate of return, the optimal R&D tax subsidy would double the private after-tax rate of return to R&D investment. For example, given a corporate tax rate of 35%, after-tax returns would equal 65% of pre-tax returns for corporations, assuming no tax subsidies or preferences. In this case, the optimal R&D tax subsidy would double the private after-tax returns to R&D investment by increasing them to 130% of pre-tax returns [2 x (1-0.35)].

Cox's analysis implied that the optimal average effective rate for an R&D tax subsidy, or a combination of such subsidies (e.g., a research tax credit combined with the treatment of research expenditures as a current business expense), was 30%. In discussing the policy implications of this finding, Cox noted that such a rate was an average and thus would not address the considerable variation among R&D investments in the difference between private and social returns. So using tax incentives to boost pre-tax returns on R&D investment by 30% across all industries would provide excessive subsidies for projects with below-average spillover benefits and insufficient subsidies for projects with above-average spillover benefits. According to Cox, lawmakers should be aware that "this imprecision is unavoidable, and its consequences are hard to assess."[34]

How do existing federal tax subsidies for R&D investment compare with Cox's assessment of the optimal R&D tax subsidy? To determine the incentive effect of then-current federal subsidies, he estimated the pre-tax and after-tax rates of return under 1995 federal tax law for a variety of hypothetical R&D projects. The projects differed in the share of R&D expenditures devoted to depreciable assets like structures and equipment, the share of R&D expenditures eligible for both expensing under IRC Section 174 and the regular research credit, and the economic lives of the intangible assets created by the investments. Cox compared the combined effect of expensing and the credit on after-tax returns to investment in capital-intensive, intermediate, and labor-intensive R&D projects producing intangible assets with economic lives of 3, 5, 10, and 20 years.[35]

Expensing has the effect of equalizing the pre-tax and after-tax rates of return on an investment, since it taxes the income earned by affected assets at a marginal effective rate of zero.[36] For the typical business R&D investment, it is likely that only part of the total cost may be expensed under IRC Section 174, as tangible depreciable assets like structures and equipment do not qualify for such treatment. Therefore, how expensing affects an R&D investment's after-tax rate of return depends on two factors: (1) the percentage of the total cost that may be expensed, and (2) the marginal effective tax rate on income earned by the assets (including labor) eligible for expensing.

The regular research credit raises the after-tax rate of return only on a portion of current-year QREs: those above a base amount. So its effect on the after-tax returns to an R&D investment depends on both the percentage of the investment's total cost that qualifies for the credit and the effective tax rate on income earned by assets eligible for the credit.

Allowing for these limitations on the benefits of expensing and the regular credit, Cox estimated that expensing and the credit together produced median after-tax rates of return ranging from 101.0% of pre-tax returns for a hypothetical capital-intensive project yielding intangible assets with an economic life of 20 years to 124.7% for a hypothetical labor-intensive project yielding intangible assets with an economic life of three years.[37] As these percentages are less than 130%, he inferred that the research tax subsidies in existence in 1995 did not increase private after-tax returns to R&D investments to the "levels warranted by the spillover benefits that are thought to be typical" for these investments.[38]

Gap between the Credit's Average Effective Rate and Its Statutory Rate

Some critics of the regular credit see its incentive effect in a somewhat different, though related, light. For them, a more important concern than the credit's potential to boost business investment in research to socially optimal levels is any differences between the regular credit's average effective rate and its statutory rate of 20%. As noted earlier, whatever differences exist from firm to firm can be ascribed largely to three of the rules governing the use of the credit.

One of the rules is the basis adjustment under IRC Section 280C(c)(1), which requires taxpayers investing in qualified research to reduce any deduction for research expenditures they take under IRC Section 174 by the amount of any research credit they claim. This adjustment effectively adds the credit to a firm's taxable income and taxes it at the firm's income tax rate. Consequently, for business taxpayers taking the credit that are subject to the maximum corporate or individual tax rate of 35%, the basis adjustment decreases the marginal effective rate of the credit from 20% to 13%. Firms have the option of computing the regular research credit at a statutory rate of 13% in exchange for leaving intact any Section 174 deduction.

A second rule is the requirement that the base amount for the regular credit cannot be less than 50% of a firm's current-year QREs. Perhaps unintentionally, the rule curtails the credit's potential benefit to established firms whose ratio of current-year QREs to gross income is more than double their fixed-base percentages, or more than double the 16% cap on the fixed-base percentage—which is to say established firms that historically have invested heavily in qualified research. Start-up firms, whose current-year ratio of QREs to gross income exceeds 6% during their first five tax years, or whose current-year ratio is more than double their fixed-base percentages in the next six tax years, also are affected by the rule. For both sets of firms, it further reduces the marginal effective rate of the credit to 6.5%.

The third rule is the exclusion of expenditures for equipment and structures and overhead costs from expenses eligible for the regular credit—even though many business research investments involve the acquisition of elaborate buildings and sophisticated equipment, and all research projects have overhead costs. In this case, the rule's effect on the marginal effective rate of the credit depends on the share of the cost of an R&D investment to which the credit does not apply. As this share rises, the credit's marginal effective rate drops, all other things being equal. For example, if expenditures for physical capital account for half of the cost of an R&D investment, then the marginal effective rate of the credit for the entire investment is half of what it would be if the entire cost were eligible for the credit. For firms subject to the 50% rule that invest in research projects where physical capital represents 50% of the total cost, the marginal effective rate could fall to 3.25%.

In addition, in a 2009 report on problems with the credit's design, the GAO brought into the analysis of the credit's marginal effective rate the impact of delays in the use of the credit. In essence, they reduce the present value of the credit, and such a reduction lowers the rate. The longer the delay and the larger a taxpayer's discount rate, the larger the rate decline. GAO estimated the marginal effective rate for all the corporations in the IRS database that claimed the credit in 2003 to 2005 and used them to compute a weighted average rate for all taxpayers. It found that the rate ranged from 6.4% to 7.3%, depending on the assumptions about the length of any delay in using the credit and the discount rate.[39]

As these considerations suggest, one of the keys to bolstering the regular credit's incentive effect is to increase its marginal effective rate. There are two ways to do so: (1) keep the current statutory rate and relax or repeal one or more of the three rules, and (2) retain the rules but raise the credit's statutory rate to offset their effects.

Cox analyzed the effects of both options on after-tax rates of return for the same hypothetical R&D investments discussed above. In the case of labor-intensive R&D projects, he estimated that 1995 research tax preferences produced median after-tax returns that were 124.7% of pre-tax returns for projects yielding intangible assets with an economic life of three years, and 115.5% for projects yielding intangible assets with an economic life of 20 years. Repealing the basis adjustment for the credit caused median after-tax returns to increase to 146.0% of pre-tax returns for assets with a three-year economic life, and 130.1% for assets with a 20-year economic life.[40] Increasing the statutory rate of the credit to 25% but retaining existing rules (including the basis adjustment) led to similar results: median after-tax returns for assets with a three-year economic life were an estimated 133.9% of pre-tax returns, and an estimated 121.9% for assets with a 20-year economic life.[41] As one might expect, increasing the rate to 25% and removing the basis adjustment led to the biggest boost in the ratio of after-tax returns to pre-tax returns: 165.8% for assets with a three-year economic life, and 143.4% for assets with a 20-year economic life.

If it is true that the optimal R&D tax subsidy should raise after-tax returns to 130% of pre-tax returns, Cox's analysis suggested that keeping the regular credit's statutory rate at the current level of 20% but eliminating or relaxing the three rules governing the credit's use might be the better policy option for strengthening the credit's incentive effect.

Non-refundable Status

The research tax credit is non-refundable. This means that only firms with sufficient income tax liabilities may benefit from the full amount of the credit claimed in a tax year. In addition, the credit is a component of the general business credit (GBC) under IRC Section 38, and therefore subject to its limitations. For firms undertaking qualified research, a key limitation is that the GBC cannot exceed a taxpayer's net income tax liability, less the greater of its tentative minimum tax under the alternative minimum tax or 25% of its regular income tax liability above $25,000.

Unused GBCs may be carried forward 20 years or back one year. Although there are some advantages to having an inventory of tax credits to apply against future or past tax liabilities, the advantages do not necessarily outweigh the disadvantages for firms investing in R&D. One disadvantage is that a business taxpayer is better off using the full amount of a credit today, rather than 5 or 10 years from now, owing to the time value of money.

Critics contend that the credit's lack of refundability can pose a special problem for small, fledgling, research-intensive firms. In recent decades, numerous commercially successful technological innovations have originated with such firms.

Many of them spend substantial sums on R&D during their first few years, while recording a stream of net operating losses. In the view of critics, a non-refundable research credit is likely to reduce the typical small, research-intensive start-up firm's prospects of survival and growth, as the firm cannot count on having access to the credit when the need for it is greatest. To remedy this problem, some advocate making the credit wholly or partially refundable for firms under a certain asset or employment size or age.[42] Other options include allowing small start-up firms that cannot use the current-year credit to sell it to other firms or use it to offset their employment taxes.[43]

Incomplete and Ambiguous Definition of Qualified Research and Difficulties in Using the Credit

Critics claim that another problem raised by the current research tax credit is the activities that qualify for it. At its core, the issue concerns the definition of qualified research and how the IRS and taxpayers interpret it in the real world of business investment in basic and applied research.

Critics argue that the statutory definition in IRC Section 41(d) and IRS regulations implementing it are vague and incomplete. This lack of clarity and finality, coupled with the complexity of the credit, the difficulty of documenting claims for the credit in a manner that passes muster with the IRS, and a lack of useful guidance from the IRS and courts, paves the way for protracted and costly disputes between taxpayers and the IRS over the validity of claims for the credit.[44] These disputes can dampen the stimulative effect of the credit in two ways. IRS audits of claims for the credit can lead to firms receiving smaller credits than they thought they were entitled to. In addition, the prospect of having a claim audited and engaging in a lengthy dispute with the IRS over its legitimacy can deter some firms that invest in qualified research from claiming the credit.

Original Definition

Under the original credit, which was in effect from 1981 through 1985, research expenditures generally qualified for the credit if they were eligible for expensing under IRC Section 174. There were three exceptions to this general rule, however: no credit could be claimed for research conducted outside the United States, research in the social sciences or humanities, and any portion of research funded by another entity. Section 174 allows business taxpayers to deduct all "research or experimental expenditures" incurred in connection with their trade or business, without defining those outlays.

The IRS filled the gap by issuing regulation 1.174-2(a), which defined research or experimental expenditures as "research and development costs in the laboratory sense," especially "all such costs incident to the development or improvement of a product." Expenditures can be considered R&D costs in the "experimental or laboratory sense" if they relate to activities intended to discover information that would eliminate uncertainty concerning the development or improvement of a product." Uncertainty exists in the R&D process when the information available to researchers does not clearly show how they should proceed in developing a new product or improving an existing one. According to the regulation, the proper standard in determining whether research expenditures qualify for expensing under Section 174 is the "nature of the activity to which the expenditures relate, not the nature of the product or improvement being developed."

Changes under the Tax Reform Act of 1986

Responding to a concern that business taxpayers were claiming the credit for activities that had more to do with product development than technological innovation, Congress tightened the definition by adding three tests through the Tax Reform Act of 1986 (TRA86).[45] Under the act, qualified research still had to involve the activities eligible for expensing under Section 174. But such activities also had to satisfy the following criteria:

- they were directed at discovering information that is "technological in nature" and useful in the development of a new or improved business component for the taxpayer;
- they constituted "elements of a process of experimentation;"
- and they were intended to improve the function, performance, quality or reliability of a business component.[46]

TRA86 defined a business component as "a product, process, computer software, technique, formula, or invention" held for sale or lease or used by a taxpayer in its trade or business. It also specified that research aimed at developing new or improved internal-use software could qualify for the credit only if it met the general requirements for the credit, was intended to develop software that was innovative and not commercially available, and involved "significant economic risk."

Subsequent IRS Guidance

In light of the significant changes made by the act, there was renewed pressure on the IRS to issue final regulations clarifying the meaning and limits of the three new tests for qualified research. But for reasons that still are not entirely clear, the IRS did not issue proposed regulations (REG-105170-97) on the tests until December 1998.

Among other things, the regulations set forth guidelines for determining whether or not a business taxpayer has discovered information that is "technological in nature" and "useful in developing a new or improved business component of the taxpayer" through a "process of experimentation that relates to a new or improved function, performance, reliability, or quality." The IRS proposed that research would meet the so-called discovery test if it were intended to obtain "knowledge that exceeds, expands, or refines the common knowledge of skilled professionals in the particular field of technology or science." At the same time, according to the proposed regulations, such a standard did not necessarily mean the credit would be denied to taxpayers who made technological advances in an "evolutionary" manner, or taxpayers who failed to achieve the desired result, or taxpayers who were not the first to achieve a certain technological advance. In addition, the IRS proposed that research would meet the experimentation test if it were to draw upon the "principles of physical or biological sciences, engineering, or computer science (as appropriate)" to evaluate "more than one alternative designed to achieve a result where the means of achieving the result are uncertain at the outset." Such an evaluation should involve developing, testing, and refining or discarding hypotheses related to the design of new or improved business components.

The release of the proposed regulations drew more criticism than praise from the business community. Much of the dissent focused on the proposed guidelines for the discovery test. A widely shared complaint was that the "common knowledge" test violated the intent of Congress and would prove burdensome and unworkable for tax practitioners because it was too subjective. Most tax practitioners and businesses that commented on the proposal urged the IRS to jettison the test.[47]

After reviewing the many comments it received and examining recent case law and the legislative history of the research tax credit, the IRS issued what was intended to be a final set of regulations (T.D. 8930) on the definition of qualified research in late December 2000. While differing somewhat from the proposed regulations, the final regulations retained the common knowledge test for determining if the information gained through research was technological in nature and useful in the development of a new or improved business component. But they clarified the application of the test by noting that the "common knowledge of skilled professionals in a particular field of science or engineering" referred to information that would be known by those professionals if they were to investigate the state of knowledge in a field of science or engineering before undertaking a research project. The final regulations also carved out a safe harbor for patents by affirming that a taxpayer would be presumed to have passed the common knowledge test if the taxpayer could prove it had been awarded a patent for a new or improved business component. They also established new standards for determining when the development of computer software for internal use qualified for the credit. Specifically, research on internal-use software was eligible for the regular credit only if it satisfied the general requirements for the credit, entailed "significant economic risk," and resulted in the development of innovative software that was not commercially available.

To the surprise of some, the final regulations aroused as much opposition within the business community as the proposed regulations. A principal concern was the IRS's insistence on retaining the discovery test. Many tax practitioners also complained that a number of the provisions in the final regulations were not included in the proposed regulations, precluding public comment on them.[48]

This second round of criticism spurred the IRS to take an unusual procedural step. About one month after the release of the regulations, the Treasury Department published a notice (Notice 2001-19) retracting them. The notice also requested further comment "on all aspects" of the suspended regulations, promised that the IRS would carefully review all questions and concerns, and committed the IRS to issue any changes to the final regulations in proposed form for additional comment.[49]

In December 2001, the IRS delivered on this promise by releasing more proposed regulations (REG-112991-01). They departed in some important ways from previous guidance. Among other things, the regulations did not include the requirement set forth in T.D. 8930 that qualified research seek to discover "knowledge that exceeds, expands, or refines the common knowledge of skilled professionals in a particular field of science or engineering." The regulations also modified the definition of the experimentation test so that it became a "process designed to evaluate one or more alternatives to achieve a result where the capability or the method of achieving that result, or the appropriate design of that result is uncertain as of the beginning of the taxpayer's research activities." The determination of whether a taxpayer engaged in such a process would be made on the basis of relevant facts and circumstances. In addition, the proposed regulations stipulated that internal-use software could not to be sold, leased, or licensed to third parties and was eligible for the credit only if it is intended to be novel in its design or applications. Tax practitioners and businesses generally approved the proposed changes.[50]

About two years later, the IRS published another set of final regulations (T.D. 9104) that was intended to clarify the definition of qualified research and certain other matters related to the credit.[51] Some analysts saw them as an attempt by the IRS to adhere to congressional intent in altering the definition of qualified research, as specified in TRA86.

The regulations noted that information is technological in nature if the process of experimentation used to discover it relies on the principles of the physical or biological sciences, engineering, or computer science. Though they discarded the discovery test included in T.D. 8930, the regulations made it clear that taxpayers would be deemed to have discovered information that is technological in nature by applying "existing technologies.... and principles of the physical or biological sciences, engineering, or computer science" in the process of experimentation.

Such a discovery would not depend on whether a taxpayer succeeded in developing a new or improved business component. At the same time, having a patent for a business component would be considered "conclusive evidence that a taxpayer has discovered information that is technological in nature that is intended to eliminate uncertainty concerning the development or improvement of (such a) component."

In addition, T.D. 9104 shed additional light on what constituted a "process of experimentation." Basically, the regulations specified that such a process had three critical aspects. First, the actual outcome must be uncertain at the outset. Second, the process must allow researchers to identify more than one approach to achieving a desired outcome. And third, researchers must use certain scientific methods to evaluate the efficacy of these alternatives (e.g., modeling, simulation, and a systematic trial-and-error investigation).

The regulations stressed that a process of experimentation is evaluative in nature, and therefore "often involves refining throughout much of the process the taxpayer's understanding of the uncertainty the taxpayer is trying to address." A taxpayer's relevant facts and circumstances should be considered in determining whether it has engaged in such a process.

Remaining Concerns

Although the regulations seemed to settle several contentious issues regarding the definition of qualified research, they did not address several other issues regarding claims for the credit that are viewed as consequential by many firms.

One issue is the circumstances under which spending on the development of internal-use software can be deemed eligible for the credit. In proposed regulations issued in 2001, the IRS stated that any costs incurred to develop such software were eligible for the credit only if the software was intended to be unique or novel and to differ in a "significant and inventive" way from previous software. But in the absence of further guidance on the meaning of "significant and inventive," disputes between IRS examiners and taxpayers over the validity of claims for the credit tied to internal-use software are more likely than not. One analyst has noted that since the release of the final regulations, the IRS has interpreted the definition of significant and inventive in a way that imposes the same requirements on the development of internal-use software that the discarded discovery test did.[52]

Another issue is the eligibility of research aimed at achieving significant cost reductions. Cost reduction is not identified in the statute as a purpose of qualified research, but the research required to lower costs can be as challenging as research done to improve a business component's reliability or performance. Some have pointed out that research that allows a product or process to deliver the same performance at a reduced cost represents an improvement in performance.[53]

In addition, tax practitioners have complained that in the wake of the strong opposition within the business community to T.D. 8930, the IRS has stopped using revenue rulings and regulations in favor of internal administrative announcements to communicate its interpretations of the IRC Section 41. These announcements, according to these critics, are sent to IRS employees in an effort to build a uniform approach to auditing claims for the credit that avoid public comment. Critics charge that these internal communications force some business taxpayers to "resort to costly litigation to determine the application of Section 41 to their facts and circumstances," undermining the credit's incentive effect.[54]

Finally, substantiation of claims for the credit remains a significant source of disputes with the IRS, curtailing its incentive effect. Concerned about the legitimacy of late or amended claims for the credit, the IRS designated "research credit claims" as a tier 1 compliance issue in April 2007.

Supporting claims for the credit typically requires subjective judgments that are subject to differing interpretations. These differences often surface in IRS examinations of claims for the credit. Examiners allegedly "routinely" deny claims because they do not strictly follow IRS's documentation standards, even though the standards never have been clarified in IRS regulations.[55]

Taxpayers are upset because the IRS expects them to provide supportive evidence without useful guidance on the required documentation standards. In its defense, the IRS maintains that it cannot audit claims for the credit unless it has detailed records linking specific expenses to specific qualified research activities. According to a 2009 GAO report, in many cases, "taxpayers settle for 50 cents on the dollar when the IRS challenges a claim."[56]

Insufficient Focus on Innovative Research Projects

Another problem with the current research credit, according to critics, is that it is not targeted at research projects with a significant potential for producing substantial economic benefits. In their view, the design of the credit makes it likely that it generates less bang for the buck in the long run than federal grants for basic and applied research in fields with broad commercial applications.

Assessing the validity of this claim is a challenge, largely because it is unclear at the outset of a research project how innovative it will prove to be. There are no known studies that undertake such an assessment. Nonetheless, the contention seems plausible in a way that might be difficult to disprove.

In general, businesses seek the highest possible return on their investments. So in selecting research projects to fund, they can be expected to assign a higher priority to projects that are likely to earn substantial profits in the short run than to projects directed at expanding the frontiers of knowledge in a scientific field that have relatively low prospects of yielding profits in the short run. This assumes, of course, that a firm has the option of investing in either kind of project or both at the same time.

Such an expectation not only seems reasonable by the logic of business investment and growth, but it is consistent with several significant trends in U.S. research spending that stretch back to the 1950s.

As Figure 1 illustrates, the federal government has long served as the major source of funding for basic research performed in the United States; from 1955 to 2008, its share of total spending (in current dollars) for this purpose was about three times the share for businesses, though the gap has narrowed somewhat since the early 1980s. At the same time, U.S.- and foreign-based companies steadily expanded their share of total funding for applied research and development performed in the United States in that period; by 2008, the business share was 88% greater than the federal share for applied research and more than five times greater for development.

These trends arguably confirm that the average firm prefers to invest much more in applied research and development than in basic research. This is hardly surprising, as the returns on investment in basic research tend to be more difficult to appropriate and more uncertain at the outset, than the returns to investment in applied research and development. The trends also lend support to the view that the credit mainly subsidizes research projects with relatively small spillover benefits, as it applies to qualified projects involving basic and applied research, as well as development.

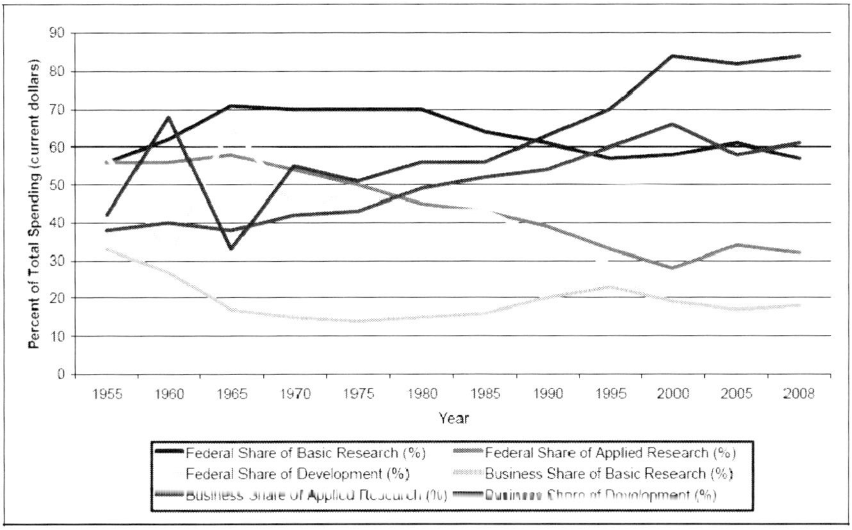

Source: National Science Foundation, Division of Science Resources Statistics, *National Patterns of R&D Resources: 2008 Data Update*, NSF 10-314, Tables 6-8.

Figure 1. Share of U.S. Spending (in current dollars) on Research and Development Held by the Federal Government and Businesses, 1955 to 2008.

To address this concern, critics recommend that Congress modify the credit so that it expressly targets investment in research aimed at developing "breakthrough products that create new product categories or innovative enhancements to existing products."[57]

Among the options are replacing the current credit with one that has a larger credit rate (say 30%) for such expenditures and transferring the authority to administer the credit to the NSF. A presumed advantage of using the NSF rather than the IRS to identify investments that would qualify for the revised credit is that the NSF has a greater supply of the expertise required to evaluate research projects for the purpose of determining which could be regarded as innovative.[58]

LEGISLATION IN THE 112TH CONGRESS TO MODIFY AND EXTEND THE RESEARCH TAX CREDIT

The research tax credit has enjoyed strong bipartisan support since its inception, and there is no evidence that the current Congress is an exception.

For over two decades, a major obstacle to extending the credit longer than a year or two, or to improving its efficacy, has been the revenue cost of doing so. If anything, this issue is even more of an obstacle in the current Congress, which has been grappling with finding politically feasible ways to reduce or eliminate current and projected future budget deficits and federal debt.

At least 12 bills to revise the research credit have been introduced in the first session of the 112th Congress. The changes they would make are summarized below.

House

H.R. 871 would permanently extend the current credit and increase the credit rate for taxpayers with more than 50% of gross receipts from domestic production activities.

H.R. 942 would permanently extend the ASC and increase its rate to 20%; it would also extend the regular credit through 2012 and then repeal it.

H.R. 1329 would make the same changes as H.R. 871.

H.R. 1693 would permanently extend the current credit and raise the rate for the ASC to 17%.

H.R. 1773 would permanently extend the current credit, increase the ASC rate to 20%, and repeal the AIRC.

H.R. 2632 would modify Section 41 of the federal tax code to create a new credit for "initial life sciences research." The regular credit would equal 40% of qualified expenses, while the ASC would equal 28% of those expenses, up to $150 million per taxpayer. The entire amount of payments for qualified contract research conducted by certain research consortia, federal laboratories, and eligible small firms would qualify for the credit. Life sciences research would qualify for the credit if it involves "the branch of knowledge or study of biology, biochemistry, biophysics, bioengineering, biotechnology, microbiology, genetics, or physiology," as it relates to human beings.

Senate

S. 155 would raise the rates for the four research credits by "bonus amounts" that depend on the share of a taxpayer's gross receipts that come from domestic production activities.

S. 239 would alter the university basic research credit so that it applies to research with specific commercial objectives or applications.

S. 361 would extend the current credit though 2016 and increase the ASC rate to 20% for tax years after 2012; the ASC rate would go up to 10% for taxpayers with at least one tax year out of the previous three without QREs.

S. 825 would permanently extend the ASC, raise its rate to 20% and 10% for tax years after 2011, and make the credit refundable for companies with 500 or fewer employees in the current tax year. It would also create an enhanced credit for domestic manufacturers that receive more than 50% of their gross receipts from domestic production activities.

S. 1410 would modify the research credit in the same manner as H.R. 2632.

S. 1577 would permanently extend the ASC, increase its rate to 20% and 10%, and repeal the current regular credit, the university basic research credit, and the energy research credit.

S. 1866 would permanently extend the ASC and increase its top rate to 20%, extend the regular credit through 2012 and then allow it to expire, and allow domestic manufacturers to claim a bonus credit if their domestic production receipts account for 50% or more of their total production gross receipts. The bonus amount rises for each 10 percentage point gain in the share of the former to the latter, up to a share of 100%.

Other Noteworthy Perspectives on the Future of the Credit

In its budget request for FY2013, the Obama Administration asks Congress to permanently extend the existing research credit and increase the rate for the ASC from 14% to 17%. The projected revenue cost for these changes is $108.5 billion from FY2013 to FY2022.[59]

In a report issued in November 2009, the Government Accountability Office (GAO) recommended that Congress consider simplifying the credit by eliminating the regular credit and establishing a minimum base amount for the ASC equal to 50% of a taxpayer's current-year QREs.[60] The report also noted that if Congress prefers to retain the structure of the existing credit, it might consider updating the base period that many companies are required to use to calculate their fixed-base percentages for the regular credit. Finally, GAO recommended that Congress consider making certain changes in the administration of the credit to reduce the compliance burden on firms and the cost to the IRS of ensuring that claims for the credit comply with existing regulations.

End Notes

[1] Linda R. Cohen and Roger G. Noll, "Privatizing Public Research," *Scientific American*, September 1994, p. 72.

[2] See, for example, Edwin Mansfield, "Microeconomics of Technological Innovation," in *The Positive Sum Strategy*, Ralph Landau and Nathan Rosenberg, eds. (Washington: National Academy Press, 1986), pp. 307-325; and John C. Williams and Charles I. Jones, "Measuring the Social Return to R&D," *Quarterly Journal of Economics*, vol. 113, no. 4, November 1998, pp. 1119-1135.

[3] For a brief discussion of these channels, see Bronwyn H. Hall, "The Private and Social Returns to Research and Development," in *Technology, R&D, and the Economy*, Bruce L. R. Smith and Claude E. Barfield, eds. (Washington: Brookings Institution and American Enterprise Institute, 1996), pp. 140-141.

[4] For more information on the Section 174 expensing allowance, see U.S. Congress, Senate Committee on the Budget, *Tax Expenditures*, committee print, 107th Cong., 2nd sess. (Washington: GPO, 2002), pp. 55-58.

[5] Office of Management and Budget, *Analytical Perspectives, Fiscal Year 2012* (Washington: GPO, 2011), pp. 66 and 367.

[6] The Emergency Economic Stabilization Act of 2008 (P.L. 110-343) repealed the AIRC for the 2009 tax year only. It has not been reinstated.

[7] See the discussion of concerns raised by the current definition of qualified research in the "Incomplete and Ambiguous Definition of Qualified Research" section of this report.

[8] U.S. Office of Technology Assessment, *The Effectiveness of Research and Experimentation Tax Credits* (Washington: 1995), p. 29.

[9] For a variety of reasons, which will be discussed in a later section of the report, the actual or effective rate of the credit is much lower than 20%.

[10] Available studies indicate that the price elasticity of demand for R&D ranges from 0.2 to 2.0, which means that a 1% reduction in the cost of R&D would raise R&D spending between 0.2% and 2%.

[11] In other words, the expenses against which the regular research credit may be claimed can equal no more than 50%of total QREs in a given tax year.

[12] The definition of a start-up firm has changed a few times since the research credit was enacted. Presently, it denotes a firm that recorded gross receipts and QREs in a tax year for the first time after 1993.

[13] Calculating a firm's base amount for the basic research credit is more complicated than calculating its base amount for the regular credit. For the basic research credit, a firm's base period is the three tax years preceding the first year in which it had gross receipts after 1983. The base amount is equal to the sum of a firm's minimum basic research amount and its maintenance-of-effort amount in the base period. The former is the greater of 1% of the firm's average annual in-house and contract research expenses during the base period, or 1% of its total contract research expenses during the base period. For a firm claiming the basic research credit, its minimum basic research amount cannot be less than 50% of the firm's basic research payments in the current tax year. The latter is the difference between a firm's donations to qualified organizations in the current tax year for purposes other than basic research and its average annual donations to the same organizations for the same purposes during the base period, multiplied by a cost-of-living adjustment for the current tax year.

[14] U.S. Congress, Joint Committee on Taxation, *General Explanation of the Economic Recovery Tax Act of 1981*, joint committee print, 97th Cong., 1st sess. (Washington: GPO, 1981), p. 120.

[15] U.S. Congress, *General Explanation of the Tax Reform Act of 1986*, joint committee print, 100th Cong., 1st sess. (Washington: GPO, 1987), p.130.

[16] For a business taxpayer in the 30% tax bracket, the rule reduced the maximum effective rate of the regular research credit from 20% to 17.5%: 20 x [1-(.5 x .30)]

[17] See U.S. Congress, Joint Economic Committee, *The R&D Tax Credit: An Evaluation of Evidence on Its Effectiveness*, joint committee print, 99th Cong., 1st sess. (Washington: GPO, 1985), pp. 17-22.

[18] Martin A. Sullivan, "Research Credit Hits New Heights, No End in Sight," *Tax Notes*, vol. 94, no. 7, February 18, 2002, p. 801.

[19] The principal barriers to measuring the social returns to R&D are developing adequate price indices for the cost elements of R&D for specific industries, specifying the time period in which to assess the productivity gains from R&D, and determining the depreciation rate for a society's stock of R&D assets. For a detailed discussion of these issues, see Bronwyn H. Hall, "The Private and Social Returns to Research and Development," in *Technology, R&D, and the Economy*, Bruce L. Smith and Claude E. Barfield, eds. (Washington: Brookings Institution, 1996), pp. 141-145.

[20] This argument assumes that government research grants to the private sector do not lead firms receiving the grants to reduce their own R&D spending by similar amounts.

[21] See Bronwyn H. Hall, *Effectiveness of Research and Experimentation Tax Credits: Critical Literature Review and Research Design*, report for Office of Technology Assessment, June 15, 1995, pp. 11-13, available at http://emlab.berkeley.edu/~bhhall/papers/BHH95%20 OTArtax.pdf.

[22] Ibid., p. 18.

[23] U.S. Congress, Joint Committee on Taxation, *Description of Revenue Provisions in the President's Fiscal Year 2004 Budget Proposal*, JCS-7-03, 108th Cong., 1st sess. (Washington: March 2003), p. 250.

[24] National Science Foundation, Division of Science Resource Statistics, *The Methodology Underlying the Measurement of R&D Expenditures: 2000 (data update)* (Arlington, VA: December 10, 2001), p. 2.

[25] This estimate assumes that all the credits claimed in each year of that decade were used immediately and were not subject to reduction because of IRS audits. Delays in the use of any credit shrinks its present value, and thus its marginal effective rate. For instance, if a taxpayer claims a research credit of $1 million, has a discount rate of 5%, and cannot use the credit for three years, then the present value of the credit drops to about $864,000. Because the top marginal effective rate for the credit is 13%, owing to the rule that any deduction of research expenditures under Section 174 must be reduced by the amount of the credit, the delay in using the credit lowers the marginal effective rate to 11.2% (13% x

0.864). Delays can occur for two reasons: time-consuming IRS audits or insufficient or no tax liability against which to apply credit in the current tax year.
A 2009 report on the design of the research tax credit by the Government Accountability Office (GAO) casts doubt on the plausibility of the assumptions underlying the estimated stimulative effect of the credit from 1998 to 2008. The report found that 44% of the "total net credits earned" in 2005 could not be used immediately and thus could be carried back one tax year or forward up to 20 tax years. It also noted that IRS data on examinations of claims for the credit by corporations with annual business receipts of $1 billion or more from 2000 to 2003 indicated that the examiners recommended changes that would have lowered the aggregate amount of credits claimed by 16.5% in 2000, 19.3% in 2001, 27.1% in 2002, and 24.5% in 2003. See U.S. Congress, Government Accountability Office, *Tax Policy: The Research Tax Credit's Design and Administration Can Be Improved*, GAO-10-136 (Washington: November 2009), pp. 14-15.

[26] The R&E tax credit has been in effect for each year between July 1, 1981, and the present except for period from July 1, 1995, to June 30, 1996, when it expired. Since July 1, 1996, the credit has not been renewed to include this period.

[27] CRS Report 96-505, *Research and Experimentation Tax Credits: Who Got How Much? Evaluating Possible Changes*, by William A. Cox, pp. 5-10. (The report is out of print. Copies may be obtained from Gary Guenther (202) 707-7742, upon request.) (Hereafter cited as Cox, *Research and Experimentation Tax Credits*.)

[28] Their effective credit rate was lower because each firm was subject to the 50-percent rule, which reduced the marginal effective rate of the credit on R&D spending above the base amount by 50%.

[29] Cox, *Research and Experimentation Tax Credits*, p. 10.

[30] Two examples are aerospace and semiconductor chip manufacturers. See McGee Grisby and John Westmoreland, "The Research Tax Credit: A Temporary and Incremental Dinosaur," *Tax Notes*, vol. 93, no. 12, December 17, 2001, p. 1633.

[31] See CRS Report 95-871, *Tax Preferences for Research and Experimentation: Are Changes Needed?* by William A. Cox. (This report is out of print. Copies may be obtained from Gary Guenther at (202) 707-7742, upon request.)(Hereafter cited as Cox, *Tax Preferences for Research and Experimentation.*)

[32] Ibid., p. 8.

[33] See, for example, Edwin Mansfield, *The Positive Sum Strategy*, pp. 309-311.

[34] Ibid., p. 9.

[35] In the case of capital-intensive projects, 50% of outlays go to structures and equipment, 35% qualify for expensing and the credit, and 15% qualify for expensing alone. In the case of intermediate projects, 30% of outlays go to structures and equipment, 50% qualify for expensing and the credit, and 20% qualify for expending alone. And in the case of labor-intensive projects, 15% of outlays go to structures and equipment, 65% qualify for expensing and the credit, and 20% qualify for expensing only.

[36] See Jane G. Gravelle, "Effects of the 1981 Depreciation Revisions on the Taxation of Income from Business Capital," *National Tax Journal*, vol. 35, no. 1, March 1982, pp. 2-3.

[37] Cox, *Tax Preferences for Research and Experimentation*, p. 15.

[38] Ibid., p. 17.

[39] GAO, *The Research Tax Credit's Design and Administration Can Be Improved*, p. 14.

[40] Ibid., p. 27.

[41] Ibid., p. 27.

[42] For further discussion of the possible benefits to small firms of making the credit wholly or partially refundable, see Scott J. Wallsten, "Rethinking the Small Business Innovation Research Program," in *Investing in Innovation*, Lewis M. Branscomb and James H. Keller, eds. (Cambridge, MA: MIT Press, 1998), pp. 212-214.

[43] Michael D. Rashkin, "The Dysfunctional Research Credit Hampers Innovation," *Tax Notes*, June 6, 2011, p. 1066.

[44] Disputes over the credit are a recurring issue in IRS audits of large corporations in manufacturing, energy, chemicals, and information technology. See Alex E. Sadler and Jennifer A. Ray, "Navigating the Research Credit," *Tax Notes*, September 19, 2011, p. 1254.

[45] See P.L. 99-514, Section 231.

[46] U.S. Congress, Joint Committee on Taxation, *General Explanation of the Tax Reform Act of 1986*, JCS-10-87 (Washington: GPO, 1987), pp. 132-134.

[47] Sheryl Stratton and Barton Massey, "Major Changes to Research Credit Rules Sought at IRS Reg Hearing," *Tax Notes*, May 3, 1999, pp. 623-624.

[48] David L. Click, "Treasury Discovers Problems With New Research Tax Credit Regulations," *Tax Notes*, March 12, 2001, p. 1531.

[49] Sheryl Stratton, "Treasury Puts Brakes on Research Credit Regs; Practitioners Applaud," *Tax Notes*, vol. 90, no. 6, February 5, 2001, pp. 713-715.

[50] For more details on the latest set of proposed regulations and reactions to them in the business community, see David Lupi-Sher and Sheryl Stratton, "Practitioners Welcome New Proposed Research Credit Regulations," *Tax Notes*, December 24, 2001, vol. 93, no. 13, pp. 1662-1665.

[51] Alison Bennett, "IRS Issues Final Research Credit Rules With Safe Harbor For Qualified Activities," *Daily Report for Executives*, Bureau of National Affairs, December 23, 2003, p. GG-2.

[52] Christopher J. Ohmes, David S. Hudson, and Monique J. Migneault, "Final Research Credit Regulations Expected to Immediately Affect IRS Examinations," *Tax Notes*, February 23, 2004, p. 1024.

[53] Michael D. Rashkin, *Research and Development Tax Incentives: Federal, State, and Foreign* (Chicago: CCH Inc., 2003), p. 87.

[54] David L. Click, "Zeal and Activity in the Arena of the Research Tax Credit," *Tax Notes*, December 15, 2008, p.1307.

[55] David Click, "Substantiating the Research Credit," *The Tax Adviser*, vol. 41, no. 4, April 2010, p. 227.

[56] GAO, *The Research Tax Credit's Design and Administration Can Be Improved*, p. 33.

[57] Rashkin, "The Dysfunctional Research Credit Hampers Innovation," pp. 1066-1067.

[58] Rashkin, The Dysfunctional Research Credit Hampers Innovation, p. 1069.

[59] Department of the Treasury, *General Explanations of the Administration's Fiscal Year 2013 Revenue Proposals* (Washington: Feb. 2012), pp. 31 and 202.

[60] U.S. Government Accountability Office, *The Research Tax Credit's Design and Administration Can Be Improved*, GA0-10-136 (Washington: November 2009), p. 39.

INDEX

D

E

F

G

M

N

O

P

Q

R

S

T

U

V

W

Y